6·12·17

THE HALIFAX EXPLOSION

John Boileau

MacIntyre Purcell Publishing Inc.

MacIntyre Purcell Publishing Inc.
194 Hospital Rd.
Lunenburg, Nova Scotia
B0J 2C0
(902) 640-3350

www.macintyrepurcell.com
info@macintyrepurcell.com

Printed and bound in Canada by Friesens
Design, illustration and layout: Denis Cunningham

Library and Archives Canada Cataloguing in Publication

Boileau, John, author
6/12/17 / John Boileau.

ISBN 978-1-77276-066-8 (hardcover)

1. Halifax Explosion, Halifax, N.S., 1917. I. Title.
II. Title: 6 December 1917.

FC2346.4.B64 2017 971.6'22503 C2017-902046-3

MacIntyre Purcell Publishing Inc. would like to acknowledge the financial support of the Government of Canada and the Nova Scotia Department of Tourism, Culture and Heritage.

Funded by the Government of Canada | Canada

NOVA SCOTIA

To the memory of those heroic men and women

—military and civilian—

who laboured tirelessly

to save the lives of their fellow citizens

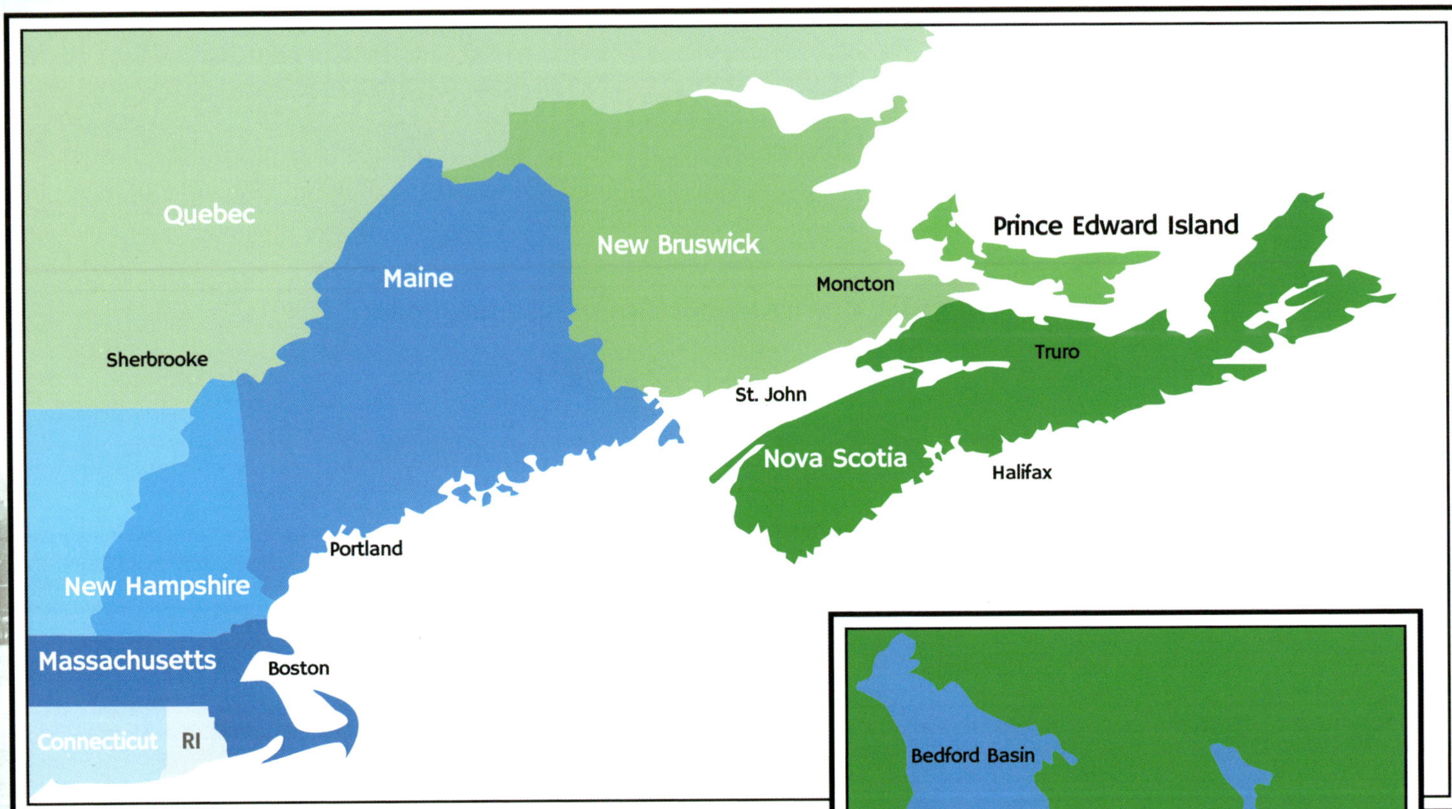

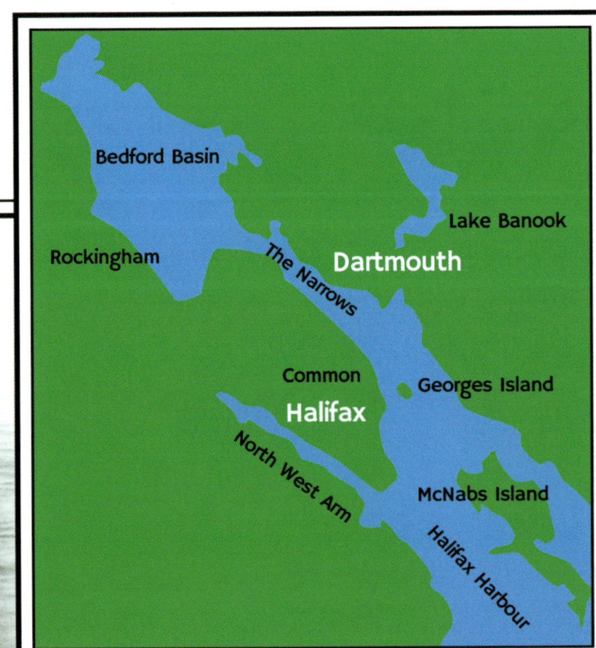

Halifax Harbour in relation to the Northeastern United States and the Maritimes.

TABLE OF CONTENTS

A view of the interior of a Mi'kmaq wigwam.

Prelude

KJIPUKTUK

It remained nameless for thousands of years, shaped and sculpted by the grinding, inexorable passage of the great glaciers as they flowed southwards over eastern North America, paused briefly, then retreated northward, repeating the cycle several times in a stately procession that encompassed eons. About 20,000 years ago, the last gigantic glacier began its northward withdrawal, dropping off bits of detritus it picked up during its southern journey.

It deposited great gobs of soil and gravel caught up in the ice—glacial till—as oval-shaped hills called drumlins. One of them would eventually be crowned with a British fortress overlooking a magnificent harbour in what is now called Nova Scotia. As the ice retreated, the sea level rose and flooded a valley that had been scoured out by glacial movement. In the process one of the world's largest and deepest harbours was created: a giant hourglass 29 kilometres (18 miles) long that ran from an outer entrance through a narrow waist and then to the head of a huge inner basin.

Other drumlins became islands, natural guardians that protected the entrance to the harbour's deep inner sanctum. By about 6,000 BC, the ice had withdrawn to its present limits.

Humans followed closely behind—first Paleo-Indians, then Mi'kmaq and finally Europeans.

The Mi'kmaq named the lengthy, deep inlet *Kjipuktuk*, or "great long harbour." Their word has come down to us today as Chebucto.

One of the favourite spots for the Mi'kmaq to set up their seasonal camps was along the shores of *Kjipuktuk*. The eastern side of the great harbour was preferred, especially where the overland river and lake route from the Bay of Fundy emptied fresh, clear water into it.

The French were the first Europeans to arrive at the great long harbour. Although they did not settle there, Samuel de Champlain noted it as *Baye Saine*, or Safe Harbour, on his map of his return journey to France in 1607. In view of later events, it was a name heavy with irony.

The British established their first permanent settlement on the western side of the harbour, on a long, oval-shaped peninsula that jutted seaward.

They named it Halifax.

And *Kjipuktuk* of the Mi'kmaq—*Baye Saine* of the French—became Halifax Harbour.

PROLOGUE

AN UNEXPECTED JOURNEY

In early December 1917—during the fourth year of the world's first truly global war—a series of seemingly unrelated events over the period of a few days culminated in the appearance of two ships at Halifax Harbour.

The arrival of these two ships led to the greatest man-made, non-nuclear explosion the world had experienced until then.

The appearance of two aging, nondescript tramp steamers in Halifax within days of each other would not normally have attracted the attention of anyone, except for the pilots who guided them in and out of the harbour and the authorities responsible for movement control—and possibly one other group.

Throughout the war, school boys played a continuing game as they attempted to identify the type and nationality of the many ships coming and going in the harbour. But boys were usually more interested in warships than ordinary civilian vessels.

One ship, *Imo*, had travelled across the Atlantic from Rotterdam and was headed for New York to pick up relief supplies for war-ravaged little Belgium. She dropped anchor in Bedford Basin on December 3. She should have departed on December 5, but was refuelled too late in the day to sail and consequently spent another night at anchor in the basin.

The second, *Mont-Blanc*, had begun her transatlantic voyage from New York just a few days before, on December 1. She arrived outside the harbour anti-submarine net late on December 5, and there she waited until the next morning because the barrier's gates were closed for the night.

Mont-Blanc's holds and decks were filled—in fact, overfilled—with a potentially devastating cargo of high explosives: picric acid, gun cotton, TNT and benzol.

The next morning—December 6—the two steamers began their unexpected journey toward each other.

As *Mont-Blanc* sailed into the harbour, *Imo* made its way out. If the initial plans of each ship's captain had unfolded as originally intended, the two vessels would likely never even have seen each other.

But they did much more than simply see each other.

At 8:45 a.m., the two ships collided while part way through the narrowest part of the harbour—predictably named The Narrows—the result of a series of navigation errors by both vessels.

Imo's bow sliced into *Mont-Blanc*'s hold and crushed a few loose grains of combustible dry picric acid in the hold, causing tiny fires and igniting benzol that had spilled and run down the open wound to the waterline from the deck above.

Naval and civilian ships proceed up Halifax Harbour towards The Narrows, 1917.

Larger fires broke out on *Mont-Blanc*.

About 20 minutes later a series of explosions followed, culminating in a gigantic blast at 9:04:35.

Within the space of a few seconds—out of a civil and military population of 70,000—1,600 human beings ceased to exist.

At least 400 more individuals were to die in the coming hours and days. Many believe the overall total is probably higher, perhaps reaching 2,500.

An unknown number were to have their lives shortened as a direct result of the disaster.

Some 500 of the dead were children.

About 9,000 were injured, many with terrible wounds—often from flying bits of glass or wood.

The blast destroyed everything within 800 metres (half a mile) and damaged buildings within 1,600 metres; a total of 1,630 structures. It caused lesser damage to another 5,000 buildings.

It left 6,000 people homeless and an additional 19,000 without adequate shelter.

Much of the north end of Halifax was flattened and many buildings in other areas of the city and its sister—Dartmouth—on the opposite side of the harbour, suffered varying degrees of damage.

In all, about one-fifth of the city was in ruins.

Coal and wood stoves knocked over by the blast quickly ignited shattered wooden houses. Soon blazes burned all over the city's north end.

The anguish and distress inflicted on the people of Halifax is difficult to imagine.

And then that night the worst winter blizzard in years hit the city, adding to the survivors' misery and hampering rescue efforts.

Scenes of destruction in the north end of Halifax after the explosion

Many wondered how this calamity would end.

Others wondered if it ever would.

The SS *Mont-Blanc* was launched in England in 1899. During the First World War, she was under French government control.

CHAPTER 1

1917

Barrington Street in 1902, photographed looking south from George Street, was Halifax's main commercial area for many years.

COMINGS AND GOINGS IN 1917

Born: **Desi Arnaz**, band leader and actor; **Ernest Borgnine**, actor; **Raymond Burr**, actor; **Arthur C. Clarke**, science fiction author; **Phyllis Diller**, comedian; **Ella Fitzgerald**, singer; **Zsa Zsa Gabor**, actor; **Indira Gandhi**, prime minister; **Dizzy Gillespie**, jazz musician; **Susan Hayward**, actor; **Lena Horne**, singer; **John F. Kennedy**, president; **Vera Lynn**, singer; **Man o' War**, race horse; **Dean Martin**, singer and actor; **Robert Mitchum**, actor; **Cyrus Vance**, secretary of state; **Caspar Weinberger**, secretary of defence; **Andrew Wyeth**, artist.

Died: **William "Buffalo Bill" Cody**, entertainer; **Mackenzie Bowell**, prime minister; **Edgar Degas**, artist; **Gilbert Ganong**, candy-maker; **Mata Hari**, spy; **Scott Joplin**, musician; **Auguste Rodin**, sculptor; **Tom Thompson**, artist; **Count Ferninand von Zeppelin**, general and airship manufacturer.

CANADA

One hundred years ago, the world was a different place. Most of the planet was ruled by empires: British, French, Spanish, Portuguese, Belgian, German, Italian, Dutch, Danish, Ottoman and Russian. Even the Americans, late-comers in the scramble for colonies, had annexed territories in the Caribbean and Pacific. There were no truly independent countries in the Caribbean, while in Africa only two nations managed to escape belonging to someone else. It was much the same picture in the Middle East and southern Asia, where few independent countries existed.

Although Canada went by the somewhat grandiose title of "self-governing Dominion," the country was not totally independent. Confederation had occurred 50 years earlier and Britain still retained some responsibilities for the country, especially in the area of foreign affairs. When Britain declared war on Germany and Austria-Hungary, Canada was automatically at war as well.

Canada was a much simpler country then. A population of barely 8,000,000 still lived largely in rural areas. The traditional family with the man as bread-winner and the woman as home-maker was the norm. Families were large, in part due to a high infant mortality rate.

Antibiotics and most immunization were unknown. Blood transfusions were only beginning. Diabetes was a death sentence.

Nearly all of today's conveniences were unimaginable. Forget about computers, televisions and smartphones. Although most Canadian homes had electric lights, few boasted indoor plumbing, a telephone or a car.

Roads and city streets were largely unpaved -- and cleared by hand in winter. Most goods moved by train and the airplane was an object of curiosity. Few people had even seen one.

A CITY IS FOUNDED —AND GROWS

In the summer of 1749, Colonel Edward Cornwallis and 2,576 settlers, soldiers and staff arrived in 13 vessels at the great long harbour, resulting in the first permanent settlement of the area. The tiny community was named in honour of Lord Halifax, President of the Board of Trade and Plantations, the organization that directed and oversaw the town's establishment. The creation of this instant community by the deliberate act of a government—rather than springing up haphazardly by chance—was unique, and the initial step in the permanent settlement of the area.

Halifax's first settlers were largely private citizens who came to Nova Scotia to obtain a grant of land on which to establish themselves and their families. Many of the settlers who arrived with Cornwallis were clearly unsuited to the daunting task of hewing their homes out of virgin wilderness. The advertisements for colonists went out too late in the season to attract the sturdy, reliable folk required and, in many cases, it was the proverbial dregs of society that came instead, looking for a free lunch ticket. Unable or unwilling to fend for themselves, by the next summer many of those who survived the first winter headed south for the milder climes and established town sites of New England.

New settlers were desperately needed to replace those who died or fled. The first "Foreign Protestants"—German, French and Swiss subjects of King George III—arrived in 1750. Many settled in Halifax's northern suburbs, while others later moved on to found Lunenburg. An expansion to the eastern side of the harbour also occurred that summer, when 353 settlers arrived on *Alderney* to establish the new community of Darmouth.

Meanwhile, other smaller communities were established along the shoreline of Bedford Basin over the years, including Bedford, Birch Cove, Rockingham and Fairview. A Mi'kmaq settlement grew at Turtle Grove on Tuft's Cove on the Dartmouth side, while a black communty known as Africville developed on the northern edge of peninsular Halifax, along the southern shore of Bedford Basin.

Colonel Edward Cornwallis, the British officer who led almost 2,600 settlers to found Halifax in the summer of 1749, made the new city the colony's capital.

POLITICS

Nova Scotian Sir Robert Borden, Canada's eighth Prime Minister, was in office from 1911 to 1920 and successfully led the country through the First World War.

The seventh session of the twelfth Parliament met from January 18 to September 20 in 1917. It passed the Soldier Settlement Act to help men returning to Canada to settle on the land. Prime Minister Sir Robert Borden made an extended visit to Britain, visiting troops at the front and attending the Imperial War Conference from March 21 to April 27. What he saw and heard from senior commanders led him to promise Britain several thousand more Canadian troops, which led directly to the passage of the Military Service Act—conscription—in August to meet his commitment.

This promise led to the most divisive election in Canadian history and a deep rift between English and French Canada. Liberals who supported conscription had already joined Borden's Conservatives to create a Unionist government in mid-October. On December 17, Canadians returned the Unionist government to power.

Universal suffrage edged forward with women given the vote in British Columbia and Ontario in April. The Military Voters' Act was passed in September, which extended the vote in federal elections to every member of the armed forces—both male and female—as well as to women relatives of servicemen. Other female advancement saw the Canada's first woman judge, Helen Emma MacGill, appointed to the bench of juvenile court in Vancouver, and Louise McKinney elected as the first member of a provincial legislature, in Alberta.

Government control over its citizens' lives also grew during 1917. On July 25, the Income Tax War Bill was introduced, imposing the first national tax on incomes, as a "temporary" measure to help finance the war. In October, strikes and walkouts were prohibited for the duration of the war, while the next month the use of grain to manufacture liquor was forbidden.

Although 1917 was the golden jubilee of Confederation, celebrations—such as they were—were subdued out of deference to soldiers living, fighting and dying in the appalling conditions of the Western Front.

(below) Sir Douglas Haig, Commander-in-Chief of the British Expeditionary Force, and Lieutenant-General Sir Arthur Currie discuss the course of the war with French President Raymond Poincaré as staff officers look on.

THE FIRST WORLD WAR

By 1917, the First World War (initially known as the European War and then as the Great War) had been raging on several fronts for nearly three-and-a-half years. The death, destruction, devastation and displacement on an industrial scale in the world's first truly global conflict were to continue for almost another two years.

The assassination of the heir to the throne of Austria-Hungary in the obscure Balkan town of Sarajevo by an even more obscure group of terrorists had drawn Britain—and therefore Canada—into the war.

By November 1916, the Canadian army overseas had grown to its final establishment of a corps of four strong divisions, described as the "most powerful self-contained force on the Western Front." The British recognized the competence of Canadian soldiers and used them as shock or assault troops to spearhead attacks. If the Germans learned Canadians moved into the line opposite them, they knew an attack would surely follow.

On Easter Monday—April 9—the Canadian Corps, assisted by the British, captured Vimy Ridge near Arras, France. It became the most celebrated Canadian victory of the war and marked the first time all four divisions attacked together.

In June, Billy Bishop was awarded the Victoria Cross for his aerial victories. He became the leading Canadian ace in the Royal Air Force, eventually shooting down 72 enemy aircraft.

Later that month, Lieutenant-General Sir Arthur Currie succeeded Julian Byng as commander of the Canadian Corps.

In his first battle as corps commander, Currie's troops captured Hill 70, near Lens, France, in what many historians regard as a more important battle than Vimy Ridge.

In October, the corps moved to Belgium to participate in the Third Battle of Ypres, better known to Canadians as Passchendaele—a term that has come to encapsulate the worst horrors of the war. In a little more than a month of fighting under the worst conditions imaginable, the corps suffered 15,654 casualties to take 5.2 square kilometres (two square miles) of mud—not far from Currie's prediction of 16,000.

"When Britain is at war, Canada is at war. There is no distinction."

Prime Minister Sir Wilfrid Laurier, 1910.

Soldiers of the 29th (Vancouver) Battalion advance across no man's land through German barbed wire and heavy fire during the Battle of Vimy Ridge, April 9, 1917.

HALIFAX AND WAR

A hospital ship discharges wounded soldiers at the Halifax docks, June 29, 1917.

As an important outpost of the far-flung British Empire, for many decades Halifax's fortunes rose and fell with Britain's wars. When the British were at war, the city prospered. When they were at peace, its economy and even its population declined due to reductions in naval and army spending. The ebb and flow of the city's fortunes usually affected the rest of the province as well, and at times people called it "Nova Scarcity." Industry and manufacturing gradually surpassed the city's traditional dependence on conflict, until the First World War began. By 1917, three years of war in Europe brought back the old wartime prosperity and turned Halifax into a boom town.

The outbreak of the war in August 1914 put Halifax back into the role she played so many times before. Although the First Canadian Contingent sailed from Quebec in October 1914, most other troops departed from Halifax—nearly 285,000 before the war ended in 1918. As a result of an influx of thousands of soldiers and sailors—and thousands of civilians—Halifax's limited nineteenth-century housing and transit facilities were heavily burdened.

This flood of mostly male humanity also brought with it another dark side: increases in prostitution, incidents of venereal diseases and the consumption of alcohol.

Halifax quickly became one of the most important cities in Canada's national war effort. Because of its significance, the harbour had to be defended from attack by sea or land. During the war, the city truly came into its own as a world-class port and naval facility. Yet, despite its contribution to the national war effort, the wartime event for which the city is most remembered is the disastrous Explosion.

Halifax, White Star and Disaster

By some strange quirk of fate, ships of the White Star Line have had an unfortunate connection with Halifax. Three ships—all ending in the suffix "ic" as was the custom of the White Star Line—brought death to the city.

On the night of April 1, 1873, the SS *Atlantic* struck an underwater rock off the nearby village of Prospect, southwest of Halifax. The loss of 562 passengers and crew was the greatest transatlantic passenger ship disaster of the nineteenth century. In all, 427 bodies were buried locally over a six-week period.

On the night of April 12, 1912, the SS *Titanic* hit an iceberg off Newfoundland and sank within three hours, resulting in the death of 1,516 passengers and crew. It was the greatest transatlantic passenger ship disaster of the twentieth century and probably the most well-known sinking of all time. Of the 2,229 passengers and crew aboard, only 713 survived. Ships recovered 337 bodies, with 128 buried at sea and 209 taken to Halifax, where 150 were buried -- the largest number of *Titanic* graves in the world.

In 1889, the SS *Runic I* was launched as a livestock carrier at the same shipyard that built *Titanic*. She was sold in 1895 and resold in 1912 and renamed the SS *Imo*. When *Imo* collided with a French ship carrying munitions in Halifax Harbour the resulting explosion killed at least 2,000 people.

HALIFAX HARBOUR AT WAR

Halifax, with a population of about 57,000, was the largest city in Atlantic Canada. It prided itself on keeping up with all the latest developments of the new century. Across the harbour the town of Dartmouth had grown to more than 7,000. Three cross-harbour ferries were hard pressed to keep up with traffic between the two communities. On both sides of the harbour, business and industry were booming as factories, foundries and mills met the demands of a wartime economy. Modern transportation and communications, schools and universities were all part of daily life.

Much of the prosperity of Halifax and Dartmouth centred on the harbour. Warships and merchant vessels were constantly departing, while formidable defences on its shores and islands bristled with coastal artillery, machine guns and searchlights. Two steel-mesh submarine nets stretched across its entrance. One ran from Ives Point on the northwest tip of McNabs Island to the Halifax shore opposite, while the other was farther up the harbour and ran from the Dartmouth to Halifax, via Georges Island. Allied and neutral ships entered through a narrow gap in them opened and closed by gate vessels, while minesweepers patrolled the outer approaches to make sure enemy subs had not laid any mines. Halifax quickly became one of the busiest ports in the world, handling approximately 15,419,000 tonnes (17,000,000 tons) of cargo annually by 1917—more than seven times the pre-war tonnages.

HMCS *Grilse* alongside at Halifax in 1916, with Royal Navy cruisers and a passenger liner in the channel.

The Pilotage Commission was key to moving traffic safely in and out of the harbour. Its 14 pilots—far fewer than required to handle the number of ships coming and going—were overworked, but largely through choice. Keeping their numbers small meant extra cash from overtime work, as the commission was essentially running a "closed shop" for many years.

Some pilots allegedly made as much as $12,000 a year—a huge salary for the time. To maintain this honey pot, the pilots strenuously objected to a naval proposal to licence additional qualified men as pilots, which created acrimony between the two sides.

Because it was wartime, and because ships entering or leaving Halifax were vulnerable to attack by German U-boats, the navy had control over all shipping in the approaches to the harbour, as well as the harbour itself.

This control was exercised by the office of the Chief Examining officer (CXO), a senior naval officer and his staff who were responsible for regulating the movement of large vessels in the harbour.

The control of movement was accomplished by the inspection of ships at an examination station off McNabs Island by an examining officer—usually a naval rating—to ensure their papers were in order. The ships were then directed to an anchorage, either at certain wharves or elsewhere in the harbour or Bedford Basin. In peacetime, such movement control was carried out by the harbour master, without the inspection aspect.

The CXO was also responsible for the operation of the submarine nets and setting the gate hours. At the time of the explosion, the CXO was Acting Commander Frederick Wyatt of the Royal Canadian Navy (RCN).

Personality Profile: Frederick Evan Wyatt

Acting Commander F. Evan Wyatt was born on September 23, 1877, in Portsmouth, England, and attended Westminster School as a Queen's Scholar from 1890 to 1894. He had civilian experience as a master of mail and passenger steamers, as well as a navigator and pilot. Wyatt also served in the Royal Naval Reserve and was placed on the Retired Officers' list in 1906. When the war broke out, he was recalled to service as a lieutenant in HMCS *Niobe*. In 1915, his superior, Captain Edward Martin, recommended him for the position of CXO, which replaced the peacetime role of harbour master. He was promoted to lieutenant-commander and, in March 1916, Admiral Charles Kingsmill recommended his promotion to acting captain. After divorcing his first wife, Madeleine Flora (Izod), he married Dorothy Manners Brookfield in 1917. He died in 1967.

EXPLOSION

At 9:04:35 on the cold, clear morning of December 6, 1917, the reality of the First World War came crashing down on Halifax.

The French ship *Mont-Blanc*, laden with a volatile cargo of munitions, exploded after colliding with the Norwegian freighter *Imo*. The explosion literally shredded *Mont-Blanc*, while *Imo* was blown onto the Dartmouth shore.

It was the largest man-made, non-nuclear explosion the world had seen up to that time.

The death, injury and sheer devastation that descended upon Halifax equalled the worst of the carnage the First World War inflicted on the battlefields of Europe.

The explosion destroyed much of north end Halifax, leaving a devastated wasteland in its wake.

CHAPTER 2

EARLY MORNING VOYAGES

The Richmond wharves, photographed in 1898. The schooner closest to the camera is tied up at Pier 6, almost in the same location as *Mont-Blanc* was when she exploded 19 years later. The arrow indicates the small dispatch station where telegraph operator Vincent Coleman worked.

DAWN OF A FATEFUL DAY

Dawn in Halifax on Thursday, December 6, 1917, held the promise of pleasant day, with two more weeks to go before the official start of winter. The sun rose at 7:39 in a cloudless sky, illuminating the still-snowless landscape, high-lighting patches of frost here and there on ground and roofs and cutting through the smoke of thousands of coal and wood fires. The air was bright, and cold, enhancing the early morning visibility.

Wisps of white haze or vapour—known as "barbers" by the locals—hung here and there close to the surface of the harbour. A barber was the result of the temperature differential between water and air. It was not uncommon at that time of year, but insufficient to hinder the range of vision of ships' crews or those on shore.

Temperatures were forecasted to range between -8°C and 4°C (17°-39°F). All in all, it was a welcome change from the mixture of rain, gusty winds and occasional flurries that had heralded the beginning of the week.

Halifax and Dartmouth residents went about their usual early morning weekday chores. Maids and housewives had earlier started fires to take away the lingering chill of night and cook breakfast; children wolfed down the last of their morning meal and completed their final preparations for another school day; businessmen and managers lingered over a final cup of tea or coffee before heading off to the office, while working men and women were already toiling or hurried along city streets to begin the day's tasks; soldiers and sailors went about their myriad duties and anyone else awake at that hour prepared for whatever the new day would bring.

No one expected that in less than two hours their lives, homes and communities would be shattered in ways that were inconceivable as they prepared for the day.

The harbour was already busy. Ferries, tugs and other small boats scurried back and forth over the water's bright surface, stevedores commenced loading or unloading cargoes alongside many of the city's wooden finger piers and ships' crews prepared to depart on their next voyage.

In Bedford Basin, an even larger assortment of vessels rode at anchor. Some of them waited to join the next convoy, others—either due to their speed or neutrality—prepared to sail unescorted. Meanwhile, harbour pilots made their way to the ships they were to guide out of the harbour.

Two ships at opposite ends of the harbour were among those getting ready to move that early December morning. One—*Mont-Blanc*—had its pilot onboard since last evening, while the other—*Imo*—was still awaiting a pilot.

Their short voyages that morning would result in the worst calamity ever to strike a Canadian city.

Ship Statistics: *Mont-Blanc*

The SS *Mont-Blanc* was built in Middlesbrough, England in 1899 at the Sir Raylton Dixon & Co. shipyard and purchased by the Société Générale de Transport Maritime. A tramp steamer in the classic "three-island" style (raised forecastle, bridge deck and poop deck), she carried a variety of cargoes around the world. Named after the most famous of French mountains, *Mont-Blanc* changed hands and port of registry several times before being purchased in December 1915 and registered at Saint-Nazaire by the Compagnie Générale Transatlantique, the state-owned corporation that took charge of much of France's wartime shipping.

Vitals:

Tonnage: 2,830 tonnes (3,121 tons)
Length: 98 m (320 ft)
Beam: 13.7 m (44.8 ft)
Depth: 4.7 m (15.3 ft)
Speed: 9.5 kts (17.6 km/h; 11 mph)
Armament: 90 mm fore cannon
95 mm aft cannon
Crew: 41

MONT-BLANC AND *IMO*

Captain Aimé Le Médec was on his first voyage in command of *Mont-Blanc*. The ship left France, bound for New York, where she first loaded provisions, machinery and explosives under a police guard at the French Line's Pier 57 on the city's North River. An additional cargo of benzol was loaded at Gravesend Bay on November 25. It was Le Médec's first experience with a shipment of explosives.

Workers made extensive renovations to *Mont-Blanc* to safely store her highly explosive cargo in the ship's eight holds. Wooden partitions separated the shipment of machinery from the explosives—as well as between each type of explosive—with copper nails used to prevent sparks.

To add to this volatile mixture, about 350 rounds of 90 and 95 millimetre shells for *Mont-Blanc*'s fore and aft guns were also onboard, a few in readiness nearby on the deck and the remainder in lower compartments.

In effect, *Mont-Blanc* was now a very large, very dangerous, floating bomb.

For safety, smoking was forbidden in almost all parts of the ship and even the carrying of matches was banned on deck. In an age when nearly all men smoked, the crew chewed tobacco to support their long-standing nicotine habit.

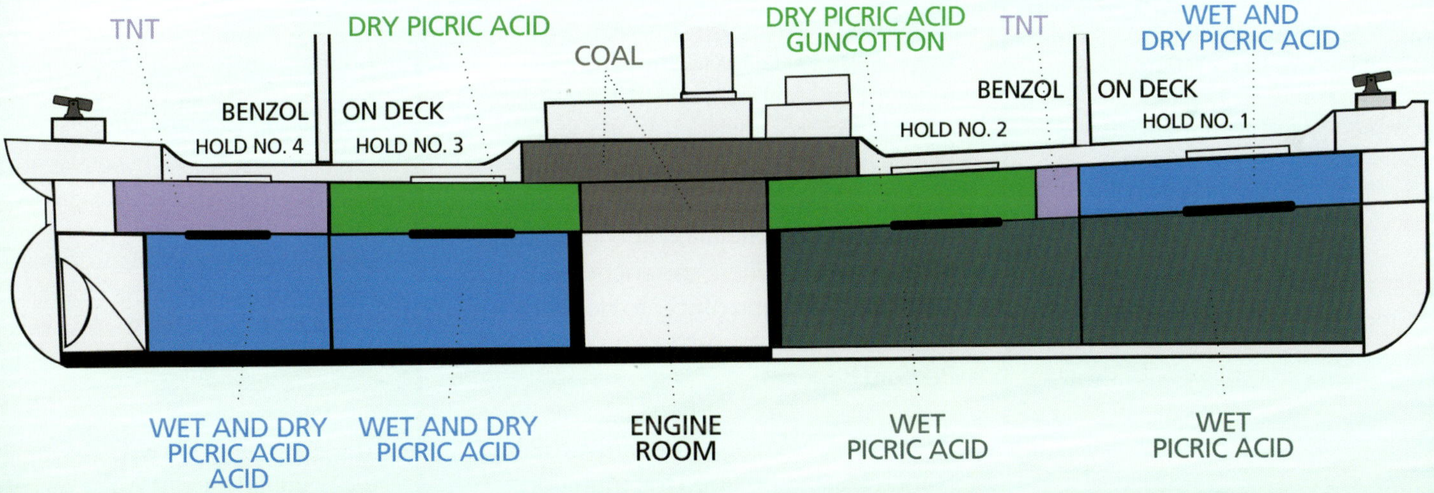

A depiction of *Mont-Blanc*'s cargo holds and their explosive contents, based on a drawing made at the inquiry by her captain, Aimé Le Médec.

Wooden panels covered the holds, which in turn were covered with tarred cloth, in effect hermetically sealing them. Lashed in the open on the fore and after decks, 494 iron drums of benzol (a high-octane aircraft fuel) completed the ship's hazardous cargo. The value of the cargo has been estimated at $3,601,290 in 1917 US dollars.

Personality Profile: Aimé Joseph Marie Le Médec

Aimé Le Médec, born in France on August 12, 1878, was captain of the French Line ships *Antilles* and *Abd El Kader* before assuming command of *Mont-Blanc*. After the trial following the explosion, Le Médec returned to France and continued working as a captain until his retirement several years later. In 1931, he received the Legion d'honneur in the grade of Chevalier. He died in 1955.

Mont-Blanc's Killer Cargo

Picric acid: 2,146.8 tonnes (2,366.5 tons), consisting of 1,602.5 tonnes (1,766.5 tons) of wet picric acid and 544.3 tonnes (600 tons) of dry picric acid.
-Picric acid, also known as Trinitorphenol or TNP, is an extremely dangerous chemical related to TNT, but it detonates faster and with more power than its cousin. It also is highly sensitive to shock, heat and friction. For picric acid to explode it must be completely dry; when kept wet with water or ethanol, it will not explode.

TNT: 226.8 tonnes (250 tons).
-Trinitrotoluene, or TNT, was invented in 1863 by German chemist Julius Wilbrand, although its potential as an explosive was not realized for several years. TNT releases less energy than gasoline, but the speed of release—its detonation velocity—creates a high-pressure blast. TNT is relatively stable and is insensitive to shock or friction.

Benzol: 223.2 tonnes (246 tons).
-Benzol is the commercial name for benzene, a highly-flammable fuel that is a by-product of the coal-refining process. When added to gasoline, it increases its burning efficiency and was used as aviation fuel.

Guncotton: 56.3 tonnes (62.1 tons).
-Guncotton is an explosive produced by steeping cotton in nitric and sulphuric acids. German-Swiss Chemist Christian Schoenbein invented it by accident in 1845, when he cleaned up a chemical spill with a cotton towel and left it by the fire to dry.

Total: 2,653.1 tonnes or 2,653,100 kilograms (2,924.6 tons or 5,849,200 pounds).

Submarine nets stretched across Halifax Harbour in two locations during the war. Because they were closed for the night on December 5, both *Imo* and *Mont-Blanc* had to wait until the next morning to begin their voyages.

Her loading complete, *Mont-Blanc* quietly stole out of Gravesend Bay at 11 p.m. on Saturday, December 1, the darkness providing at least the comforting illusion of cover. Le Médec's orders directed him to Halifax, where it was possible he might join a transatlantic convoy. His slow speed meant it was highly unlikely he would be accepted for a convoy however, and he would have to make the crossing to his intended destination of Bordeaux on his own.

Apart from a two-day northwest gale, the voyage to Halifax passed without incident and on December 4 a crewman sighted the coast of Nova Scotia. Late the next day, *Mont-Blanc* arrived off the mouth of Halifax Harbour and steamed slowly to the examination anchorage at McNabs Island, where she anchored to await an examining officer to clear her passage up the harbour to a mooring in Bedford Basin.

Before an examining officer arrived, Pilot Francis Mackey boarded the munitions-laden ship at about 4:30 p.m. He had just piloted *Kentucky* out of the harbour and *Mont-Blanc* was his next assignment. Le Médec greeted him warmly. The captain emphasized that no matches or any other open flames were allowed anywhere on the deck.

The harbour's anti-submarine nets were already closed for the night. *Mont-Blanc*, her crew and cargo would have to sit outside the nets all night in a vulnerable position—a prospect that probably did not sit well with all aboard the ship. Mackey remained aboard *Mont-Blanc*.

Red Flag? — Red Herring!

Many books and articles about the explosion state *Mont-Blanc* was not flying a red flag (actually a swallow tail burgee), as she was required to do under international regulations, to indicate a dangerous cargo—in this case, explosives. This point is then used to place at least some blame for the explosion on the French vessel.

In fact, a red flag was not flown by ships in transit during the First World War. At the time, a red flag only had to be flown by a ship when she was in port loading or discharging dangerous cargo, which could be anything from fuel to munitions.

Personality Profile: Francis Mackey

Francis Mackey (pronounced Mackie) was born on November 1, 1872, in Ketch Harbour, Nova Scotia and began his pilotage apprenticeship in 1893. He passed his second-class pilot's licence two years later, received his first-class licence in 1898 and his coasting trade master's certificate the next year. Mackey, who had married Lillian Wrayton on August 29, 1900, lived on Robie Street, near the Halifax Common. In 1917, he was a 45-year-old experienced pilot with a flawless record of 24 accident-free years. Reputedly an immaculate dresser, he claimed to know every rock and bend of land around the harbour. Although he was cleared by the courts, he was denied his pilot's licence by the federal government. After a four-year fight it was restored, but with no compensation for wrongfully-lost wages. Mackey retired in 1937 with an annual pension of $1,600. He died on December 31, 1961.

Meanwhile, at the other end of the harbour, just inside the entrance to Bedford Basin, *Imo*'s captain, Haakon From, had been waiting all day for a delivery of coal so he could continue his transatlantic voyage eastward. When the coal finally arrived, it was too late in the day to sail because the anti-submarine nets were closed -- the same problem that delayed *Mont-Blanc*'s voyage through the harbour and into Bedford Basin.

The Belgian Relief Commission had chartered From's ship to sail to New York City and pick up much-needed emergency supplies for civilians in the battle-weary little country that had been divided by Allied and German trenches slicing through the countryside of Flanders. Large red letters along each side proclaimed "BELGIAN RELIEF," in an attempt to discourage attacks against a humanitarian target by German U-boats.

Imo carried no cargo; she was travelling in ballast, which made her harder to control, especially at low speeds.

Harbour pilot William Hayes boarded *Imo* around mid-afternoon, spoke with Captain From about departing the next morning and then returned to shore for the night, promising to come back early the next day. When Hayes returned on the morning of December 6 he boarded *Imo* just as the crew were heaving up the anchor.

A few minutes later, at about 7:30 a.m., Captain From received a signal from HMCS *Acadia*, the guard ship at the entrance to Bedford Basin, that he was cleared to leave. From, already chaffing over an 18-hour delay, ordered *Imo* to get underway immediately. On the open bridge were Captain From, Pilot Hayes and Chief Officer Ingvald Iverson, with John Johansen at the helm.

According to Johansen, *Imo* left her anchorage at a speed of around two knots.

"Pretty well, yes. Some of the pebbles I might not know."

Pilot Francis Mackey, in response to a question about how well he knew the harbour shoreline during the explosion inquiry.

(below) A rare photograph of *Mont-Blanc*, which was originally taken to show the tugboat towing her out of Le Havre Harbour, France.

Ship Statistics: *Imo*

The SS *Imo* began life as *Runic I* at Harland & Wolff in Belfast on January 1, 1889. she was built to carry cargo—mostly livestock—plus 12 passengers. In May 1895, she was sold to the West Indies and Pacific Steamship Line and rechristened *Tampican*. Four years later, in December 1899, *Tampican* was transferred to Frederick Leyland & Co. along with the rest of the fleet. In 1912, the Southern Pacific Whaling Company purchased the vessel as a whaling supply ship. She was named *JMO* after the initials of the senior owner of the company—Johan Martin Osmundsen—but people started calling the ship *Imo* and the name stuck. Operating out of Oslo, Norway (known as Kristiania at the time), in 1917 she was chartered by the Belgian Relief Commission to carry supplies to war-ravaged Belgium.

Vitals:

Tonnage: 4,574 tonnes (5,043 tons)
Length: 131.24 m (430.58 ft)
Beam: 13.77 m (45.17 ft)
Depth: 9.22 m (30.25 ft)
Speed: 12 kts (22 km/h; 14 mph)
Armament: nil
Crew: 40

A TRAGEDY IN THE MAKING

At the other end of the harbour, the navy opened the gate in the submarine net at about 7:30 a.m. Although Captain Le Médec was anxiously waiting for this to occur, *Mont-Blanc* was not the first ship through the gate that morning. She was the SS *Clara*, an American cargo ship that was shortly to play a part in the unfolding tragedy.

Ship Statistics: *Stella Maris*

Stella Maris ("star of the sea") was originally built as the steam-powered wooden gunboat and minesweeper HMS *Starling* in England in 1882. She was later converted into a tugboat and purchased by the Halifax Trading & Sealing Co. Registered in Saint John, New Brunswick, at the time of the explosion she was under charter to the RCN.

Vitals:

Tonnage: 207.7 tonnes (229 tons)
Length: 37.9 m (124.5 ft)
Beam: 7.2 m (23.6 ft)
Depth: 3.7 m (12.2 ft)
Crew: 24

(above) Halifax in 1900, looking north along the rail line from the grain elevators at Pier 2, with the naval Dockyard in the middle distance on the right and the Acadia Sugar Refinery in the far distance in the middle. The north end district of Richmond climbs the slope to the left of the refinery.

It was not until the publication of *The Halifax Explosion and the Royal Canadian Navy: Inquiry and Intrigue* by John Griffith Armstrong in 2002 that *Clara* was tentatively named; and not until 2014 that Joel Zemel positively identified the ship in *Scapegoat: the extraordinary legal proceedings following the 1917 Halifax Explosion*. Before then, most books and articles simply referred to an "unknown American tramp steamer," a "mystery ship" or some similar term to describe the vessel.

Mont-Blanc followed *Clara* thorough the gate and proceeded up the harbour at a speed of four knots, below the maximum harbour speed of seven knots. After he sped up to clear the cross-harbour ferries, Mackey next ordered "half speed (about four knots), then later slow."

Personality Profile: Haakon From

Haakon From, 47, was from Sandefjord, Norway. A former whaler who had voyaged to Antarctica twice, he spent more than 25 years at sea, the last 12 as captain. He was described as a man generally of jovial spirit and even temperament and spoke fluent English. The Belgian Relief Commission chartered *Imo* in 1917 and the ship made several transatlantic crossings in safety before arriving at Halifax in early December.

Second Lieutenant Joseph Levesque from *Mont-Blanc* agreed, and noted his ship never exceeded three or four miles an hour (about 2.5 to 3.5 knots) at any time that morning.

With a number of ships anchored near the northern mouth of the Narrows, Johansen had to weave *Imo* through them before he could enter the Narrows proper. The task was made more difficult as his unladen vessel was riding high in the water.

Routes of ***Imo*** and ***Mont-Blanc*** on the morning of **December 6, 1917**, after leaving overnight anchorages.

Area of total devastation

Area of severe damage

Stella Maris began her career as a Royal Navy wooden gunboat and minesweeper in 1882 before later conversion to a tugboat.

According to *Imo*'s chief engineer, Lewis Skarre, when his ship cleared the others riding at anchor, he was ordered to make full speed ahead and got up to approximately six knots. In fact, *Imo*'s speed was likely more than seven knots, as more than one witness claimed they noticed "quite a foam at her bow."

The first ship *Imo* encountered in the Narrows was *Clara*, piloted by Edward Renner. Renner had been proceeding up the Halifax shore, contrary to regulations, as he should have been on the Dartmouth side and remained there.

According to Renner, at a distance of four or five ship's lengths apart, *Imo* "blew one, and I answered him with two and he answered me with two." By this exchange of whistles, the two pilots agreed to pass starboard to starboard, rather than the regulatory port to port. Renner may have decided to do this because it would make it easier for his ship to anchor on the western side of Bedford Basin, her eventual destination.

Whatever the reason, both ships were now performing the nautical equivalent of driving on the wrong side of the road, with *Imo* in the Dartmouth channel as she proceeded through the Narrows.

As the two ships passed each other—now not more than a ship's length apart—Renner hailed Hayes by megaphone and told him another ship was behind him coming up the harbour. Contrary to other witnesses, the *Clara* pilot estimated that *Imo* was not making much faster than five knots at the time.

The tug *Stella Maris* under Captain Horatio Brannen departed the Drydock on the Halifax side at 8:15 that morning, towing two scows, one behind the other, that were filled with ashes from naval ships to be dumped in Bedford Basin. The tug was in mid-channel when some of the crew, including the wheelsman, Walter Brannen—the captain's son—and second mate William Nickerson spotted *Imo* moving towards them.

According to Nickerson, Captain Brannen claimed "she was going as fast as any ship he ever saw in the harbour." Nickerson also said he could see foam at *Imo*'s bow and estimated her "to be making eight or 10 miles an hour" (seven to more than eight and a half knots); too fast for the Narrows. Walter Brannen estimated her speed to be "approximately five or six knots."

To avoid a collision, Captain Brannen quickly veered back towards the Halifax shore and *Imo* passed by the 122-metre (400 feet) length of tugboat and its trailing barges at a distance of 140 to 180 metres (150 to 200 yards).

Although he was unsure of the time he received them, the next orders *Imo*'s Chief Engineer Skarre recalled getting from the bridge were "dead slow and half speed and dead slow and half speed, and several different orders." This was corroborated by helmsman Johansen. Once safely past *Clara* and *Stella Maris*, he stated *Imo* was moving "very slowly—barely moving."

Unfortunately, *Imo* also stayed to port, close to the Dartmouth shore—in effect still driving on the wrong side of the road—instead of heading back to her proper channel near the Halifax side.

And, just as so often happens on land, driving this way led to an accident—one of the worst the world has ever seen.

CHAPTER 3

COLLISION COURSE

DEADLY BLUNDER

Through the early morning haze hanging over the harbour, the men on the bridges of *Imo* and *Mont-Blanc* saw each other's ships at about 1,600 metres (one mile) or so. Pilot Mackey stared—dumbfounded. He knew William Hayes piloted *Imo* and could not believe his friend would allow such a flagrant violation of the rules.

Compounding the confusion were the earlier whistles sounded by *Imo* and *Clara* when they agreed to pass to starboard, which some witnesses believed were part of the exchange of whistles between *Imo* and *Mont-Blanc*. Although witness testimony after the explosion gave conflicting accounts of the number of whistles blown and which ship blew them, a general consensus did emerge.

Le Médec gave *Mont-Blanc*'s whistle a short sharp blast: "I am directing my course to starboard."

As the first captain to blow his whistle, this put Le Médec in control of the situation, to which the second captain was to respond appropriately.

Incredibly, *Imo* responded with two blasts from her whistle: "I am directing my course to port."

After *Mont-Blanc* blew one blast, Le Médec immediately ordered dead slow and moved closer to the Dartmouth shore, now only about 90 metres (100 yards) away.

Mackey saw foam at *Imo*'s bow and thought she was moving in excess of the speed limit—"at least seven knots." Yet, according to *Imo*'s Skarre and Johansen, by that point *Imo* was proceeding dead slow.

To be sure they had understood *Imo*'s signals, Le Médec and Mackey repeated their single whistle blast: "I REPEAT I AM DIRECTING MY COURSE TO STARBOARD." *Imo*'s two-blast response echoed her first: "AND I REPEAT I AM DIRECTING MY COURSE TO PORT."

Astonished on hearing the second two-whistle blast from *Imo* at a distance he estimated as 150 metres (165 yards), Le Médec ordered the helmsman to turn farther to the right and had *Mont-Blanc*'s engines stopped. His ship was about now only 60 to 70 metres (65 to 76 yards) from the Dartmouth shore. When he realized the vessels would probably collide, Le Médec quickly sounded two blasts of his own and ordered his helmsman to turn *Mont-Blanc* hard to port toward the Halifax shore, causing her to cross *Imo*'s bow.

Although her engines were stopped, the weight of *Mont-Blanc*'s cargo left her with some forward movement. The ship "obeyed completely at once."

Some of *Mont-Blanc*'s surviving crewmen in Halifax.

The explosion blast cloud towers high into the sky. At its base lay more than 10,000 dead, dying and injured—and a city in ruins.

At the same time, Captain From blew three short blasts, signalling his move to full astern. This move swung *Imo*'s bow to starboard due to a phenomenon mariners call "transverse thrust," the force generated by the rotation of *Imo*'s "right-handed" propeller.

Additionally, even though full astern was applied to *Imo*'s steam engine and despite her lack of cargo, her bulk left her with enough headway to continue forward.

This unfortunate coincidence of actions—either of which by itself might have prevented a collision—sealed the fate of the two ships.

Collision became unavoidable.

Confusingly, *Imo*'s Chief Engineer Skarre testified the last orders he received before the collision were "full stop and full speed astern." This was followed again by "full stop and full speed astern," with "several minutes between the two reverses," perhaps "three or four minutes." But Skarre was in the engine room until after the collision, and had no idea where he was in relation to *Mont-Blanc*, the land, the time or any other reference point.

Le Médec also blew three whistles for full speed astern, perhaps in a last-second attempt to soften the inevitable blow.

Both ships' engines were now reversed, but their propellers had not yet dug into the water and the vessels were still going forward. As if in slow motion, the sharp bow of the bigger and higher *Imo* sliced into *Mont-Blanc*'s steel plating in the area of her No. 1 Hold. Although Skarre said he felt the shock of the collision "very lightly" in the engine room, *Imo* had penetrated to a depth of three metres (nine feet). This opened up a gash in the French ship's bow and swung it towards Richmond's Pier 6.

It was about 8:45 a.m.

The damage to *Mont-Blanc* was not severe, but the force of the impact crushed some loose grains of dry picric acid, which burst into mini-fires. It also toppled some of the barrels stacked topside, where they leaked highly flammable benzol across the deck and down into the open wound caused by *Imo*.

(above) In 2010, Canada Post issued a two-stamp set in honour of the centennial of the Royal Canadian Navy. The stamp on the left features HMCS *Niobe* and one of her sailors, while the one on the right depicts HMCS *Halifax* and a contemporary female sailor.

(above) The SS *Imo* began her career in Ireland as *Runic I* in 1889, became *Tampican* in 1895, *Imo* in 1912 and *Guvernøren* in 1920.

This photograph of *Middleham Castle* (left) and *Picton* was taken a few moments after the explosion by James Russell, a 25-year-old junior wireless operator aboard the armed patrol and training vessel *Cartier*, located off Dockyard Pier 3. Fires burn on shore, while the Acadia Sugar Refinery lies in a smouldering heap in the centre.

FIRE!

As *Imo* backed off, the steel of her prow scraped along the broken hull plates of *Mont-Blanc*.

Sparks from this steel on steel friction added to the tiny bursts of flame from the dry picric acid and together they ignited benzol that had run down to the water line.

Wisps of white smoke materialized, initially thought by some spectators to be escaping steam.

Then a gust of black smoke appeared.

Seconds later bright red-orange flames could be seen through the dark smoke.

The fire spread quickly and *Mont-Blanc*'s forecastle was soon swallowed in flames. Thick clouds of oily, black smoke and bursts of geranium-coloured fireballs rose high into the still morning air, attracting the attention of the curious and the concerned on shore.

As the fire on *Mont-Blanc* spread, some barrels of benzol exploded with a loud bang, scattering pieces of metal across the deck, while others whizzed up into the sky like rockets.

While Captain From tried to turn *Imo* around and proceed back into Bedford Basin, Captain Le Médec on *Mont-Blanc* had to make a life-or-death decision. Based on the volatility of his cargo he had few options.

He could try to fight the fire.

He could try to scuttle the ship where she was.

He could try and beach on the Dartmouth shore.

He could try to get the ship to open water.

Realizing the futility of these actions, he came to a rapid conclusion only two minutes after the collision.

(below): The cap of a Canadian Pacific Steamship Line officer bore the red and white checkerboard image of the line's flag.

"STOP ENGINES —ABANDON SHIP!"

The Acadia Sugar Refinery, pictured in 1911, was the tallest building in Canada east of Montreal. At the time of the explosion it was not in operation, although many spectators had crowded inside to watch *Mont-Blanc* burn as she drifted toward Pier 6.

Sailors quickly lowered two lifeboats over the side and the crew rowed furiously toward the Dartmouth shore, directed by Mackey to a small shingle beach at Tuft's Cove about 400 metres (a quarter mile) away. As they neared the beach, the pilot saw *Hilford*, a tug chartered by the Royal Navy (RN), which he had noticed in the harbour earlier.

When the tug was about 180 metres (200 yards) away, Mackey recognized the figure of Lieutenant James Murray on her deck. Murray, a former captain of the *Empress of Britain*, was sea transport officer and one of the few Canadians on the staff of Rear-Admiral Bertram Chambers, the port convoy officer.

Mackey stood up in the lifeboat, waved frantically to attract Murray's attention and shouted that the ship was about to explode. When the officer gave no indication he saw or heard Mackey, the pilot repeated his warning. This time, Mackey thought Murray might have seen him, but then the tug turned toward the Halifax shore and he lost sight of the officer.

By now, *Mont-Blanc*'s two lifeboats had reached the beach and the sailors scrambled out of their boats. Le Médec told them to run into a small wood a short distance uphill from the beach.

As they scrambled to safety, they waved frantically and yelled to those watching the flaming vessel to run away.

But no one understood their mad gesticulations—and they shouted their warning in French.

Lieutenant Murray was responsible for liaison between the port convoy office and all merchant ships at Halifax scheduled to sail in convoy. Before the collision, he was aboard *Hilford* in the harbour, reported by Mackey as "coming out from the western side going around my stern." As the tug "was not in my way," the pilot paid little attention to her.

All available evidence points to the fact that Murray was one of a handful of people who knew the deadly cargo carried aboard the French vessel. Shortly after the fire started aboard *Mont-Blanc*, he ordered *Hilford*'s captain to make for his office at Pier 9. Murray planned to telephone a warning to his superior and advise others there was an explosives-laded ship on fire in the Narrows.

James Murray rose to be captain of the Canadian Pacific Steamships Line's *Empress of Britain*. During the war, as Lieutenant Murray, Royal Naval Canadian Volunteer Reserve, he was Halifax's sea transport officer.

SPECTATORS

Meanwhile, on shore the number of spectators had increased dramatically. Large billows of thick, black smoke led most observers to believe there was an oil tanker on fire, which they assumed did not pose any particular danger to them.

Longshoremen, labourers and ships' crews working on the waterfront stopped to stare at the fascinating spectacle unfolding before them, to be quickly joined by hundreds of others. Inside their Richmond homes in Halifax's north end, housewives and children were drawn to their windows or stepped out into the cool December air to join spectators already there. Factory and office workers, businessmen and managers did the same at their places of work.

It was like some gigantic fireworks show—all for free.

Charles Duggan Jr. always felt at home on the water. A ferry pilot like his father, he saw the collision and jumped in his launch to see if he could help. As he sped across the harbour, he noticed *Mont-Blanc*'s crew abandon their ship and row frantically toward the Dartmouth shore.

Duggan carried on, worried there might be someone left on the burning vessel, but cut his engine when he could feel the heat of the fire on his face.

When he saw *Stella Maris* and the whaler from the RN cruiser HMS *Highflyer* heading toward the burning ship, Duggan assumed they had the situation in hand and and restarted his engine. Just as he came about, he heard the first of a series of explosions and turned his head to see barrels on *Mont-Blanc*'s deck shoot into the air, burst into a cloud of smoke and explode into a fireball with a roar.

Suddenly apprehensive, he opened up his throttle and headed for the Dartmouth shore at top speed.

As he did so, he heard a second and third explosion follow in quick succession.

Witnesses reported as many as 10 of these small explosions as barrels of benzol blew up.

At the Royal Naval College of Canada, situated in the former British naval hospital in the north end of the Dockyard, someone shouted to come and look at the great cloud of smoke rising above the harbour, which had interrupted the cadets' morning routine. Crowding around a ground floor window, the cadets watched in fascination as the burning *Mont-Blanc* headed towards the Halifax shore.

Then she disappeared out of view behind the eight-story bulk of the Acadia Sugar Refinery. But the rising column of smoke could still be seen, punctuated now and then by shooting flames.

Mont-Blanc, abandoned and shrouded in smoke and fire, drifted toward the Halifax shore. Carried by the harbour current, she was headed in the direction of the Richmond's wooden piers, about 450 metres (1,500 feet) away.

The protected cruiser HMS *Highflyer* had been reduced to a training ship before the First World War, but was recalled to active service when the war broke out and escorted convoys from Halifax to Britain.

VALIANT SEAMEN

HMCS *Niobe*, a former Royal Navy protected cruiser, became one of the first two warships of the Royal Canadian Navy when that service was founded in 1910.

Crews from three of the several ships in Halifax Harbour that day played a major part in attempting to assist with the situation aboard *Mont-Blanc*. Despite their valiant attempts, the men aboard *Stella Maris*, *Highflyer* and *Niobe* could do nothing—and suffered dearly for their courage.

As a result of her close call, *Stella Maris* was near the scene of the collision when it occurred. Captain Brannen quickly ordered his son to rig a hose in the tug's stern, while he turned and headed for the Halifax side to anchor the two unwieldy scows he was towing. Then Brannen headed for *Mont-Blanc*, now engulfed in flames and grounded bow first next to Pier 6.

HMCS *Niobe*, permanently moored in the Dockyard, about 640 metres (700 yards) away from Pier 6, was the first ship to give the alarm after collision.

First Officer Lieutenant-Commander Allan Baddeley sent *Niobe*'s steam pinnace with six volunteers—Stoker Petty Officer Edward Beard and five seamen—under Acting Boatswain Albert Mattison, to see if they could help the stricken vessel.

Aboard *Highflyer* anchored in mid-stream, Captain Herbert Garnett saw the fire from the bridge of his ship. Although unaware of the burning ship's cargo, he inherently knew the situation could quickly become extremely dangerous. He sent Acting Commander Tom Triggs and Lieutenant James Ruffles—both volunteers—in *Highflyer*'s whaler to see if anything could be done to assist.

Horatio Brannen had been going to sea since he was a young boy. At the time of the explosion, he was captain of the tug *Stella Maris*.

Halifax Fire Chief Edward Condon poses at the wheel of his car, a 1911 McLaughlin Buick roadster. Seated beside him is Fire Board Chairman and Controller, John Hines.

The Royal Naval College of Canada opened in 1911 in the former Royal Navy hospital at the north end of the Dockyard.

There were five sailors in the whaler with Triggs and Ruffles: Leading Seaman Claude Rushen and Able Seamen James Dowling, Samuel Prewer, Joseph Murphy and William Becker. They pulled with a will toward *Mont-Blanc*, at the time drifting helplessly about 1,200 metres (three quarters of a mile) away.

By the time the whaler got near *Mont-Blanc*, now engulfed in 30-metre- (98-feet-) high flames, the ship had grounded onto the harbour bottom on south side of Pier 6. Only the forward part of the vessel touched the pier, leaving a gap between the stern and the wharf.

Stella Maris was already there and had tried to squeeze into the space between the stern and pier, but backed off due to the intensity of the fire. Brannen and his crew valiantly—and vainly—played their small, single hose on the roaring flames from what Brannen's son estimated was 45 metres (50 yards) away.

It proved useless.

Then the tide came in and forced *Mont-Blanc*'s stern against the pier as well. Even then, a considerable length of the ship projected beyond the end of the pier, maybe "a quarter of the ship," according to Nickerson.

As *Stella Maris* reversed, Triggs came alongside in *Highflyer*'s whaler and boarded the tug to confer with Brannen for about "four or five minutes." What they said to each other is unknown, but in the end, they must have decided that nothing could be done to fight the fire, as the next action saw *Stella Maris* tow the whaler—backwards—about halfway to *Imo*, likely so Triggs could assess the damage to the ship.

When *Stella Maris* was on her way back to *Mont-Blanc*, *Niobe*'s steam pinnace came out from Pier 6 and hailed the tug. Acting Boatswain Mattison had already sent two of his sailors aboard *Mont-Blanc*. Due to the scorching heat emanating from the burning vessel's metal hull, they had climbed slowly up the port ladder—left dangling when *Mont-Blanc*'s crew abandoned their ship—to avoid touching the hot steel.

As Brannen and Mattison conferred, the *Niobe* sailor suggested the best they could hope to do would be to pull *Mont-Blanc*'s stern away from the pier. That way, the fire department could handle the now-burning pier, while other ships with proper fire-fighting equipment could deal with the burning vessel.

Mattison's two sailors already aboard *Mont-Blanc* would be able to secure the hawser to her stern so *Stella Maris* could pull her away from the pier.

Brannen agreed, but after the five-inch cable was passed up, the two seamen decided it would not be strong enough to do the job; they needed the heavier 10-inch one.

Brannen sent Nickerson below to get the heavier cable.

Meanwhile, the Norwegian vessel, sitting high in the water due to a lack of cargo and moving at a slow speed, was difficult to steer. After Pilot Hayes spent about 15 minutes alternating between going forward and reversing in an unsuccessful attempt to return to Bedford basin, he ordered *Imo* to head out to sea.

Taken a few moments after the explosion, this is the only known image that shows the remnants of the blast itself. The bottom of the cloud blankets the Halifax waterfront off to the right, while the spit of land on the left is immediately south of today's A. Murray MacKay Bridge, the location of the former Shannon Park. It was taken about two kilometres metres (1.25 miles) from the explosion, either from a boat in Bedford Basin or more likely somewhere along its eastern shore.

(opposite centre) Rear-Admiral Bertram Chambers of the Royal Navy was Halifax's port convoy officer at the time of the explosion. In 1920, he wrote a lengthy anonymous account of the disaster in the journal *The Naval Review*.

ON SHORE

Halifax firemen proudly pose outside the West Street Fire Station with their first motorized apparatus, which they christened *Patricia*. Chief Condon and Board Chairman Hines stand on the left.

While this action took place in the harbour, on land others did their part to deal with the fire.

Minutes after the fire started on *Mont-Blanc*, Captain Fred Pasco, temporary captain superintendent of the Dockyard in the absence of Captain Edward Martin, was called at Martin's home in the Dockyard, where he was living temporarily, and informed of the blaze. He immediately tried to telephone Lieutenant Murray, but instead made contact with Lieutenant Poole, Murray's second-in-command.

With the Dockyard and all its resources under his temporary command, Pasco ordered Poole to send the tugs *W.H. Lee*, *Gopher*, *Musquash* and any other available ones with pumps to the burning vessel as quickly as possible.

In his Barrington Street grocery store across the road from Pier 6, Constant Upham watched the spectacle of the burning ship—and now the burning pier—unfold before his eyes. As the seriousness of the blaze finally hit home, he called several nearby fire halls from his telephone—one of the few private ones in Richmond. At the same time—shortly before 9 o'clock—someone else rang the bell from nearby Box 83 and the alarm was transmitted across the city.

Firemen sprang into action at four stations: West, Brunswick and Gottingen Streets and Quinpool Road.

Horse-drawn vehicles rushed toward the fire, as did a 1912 American LaFrance pumper truck—nick-named *Patricia* by the firemen. *Patricia* was Halifax's—and Canada's—first motorized piece of firefighting equipment. Fire Chief Ed Condon and his deputy, William Brunt, set off in the official car behind *Patricia*.

The motorized pumper arrived first at the pier, its wooden pilings and sheds now in flames from the fire raging on *Mont-Blanc*.

Firemen rolled out a hose and attached it to a nearby hydrant. Once Condon pulled up behind them, he ordered Box 83 rung again, sounding a general alarm for all Halifax's fire stations.

Meanwhile, the tug *Hilford* with Lieutenant Murray aboard approached Pier 9. On arrival, it appears he put a sailor ashore from the tug to go to the crowded Richmond Station of the Canadian Government Railway (CGR) and its rail yards, only a short distance above Pier 9. The sailor was to warn anyone he could about the explosives and get them to evacuate.

The sailor dutifully ran to the outer office of the railway yardmaster, where he encountered chief clerk William Lovett and train dispatcher Vincent Coleman at work. Sometime before 8:50 a.m., he warned them of *Mont-Blanc*'s deadly cargo of high explosives. Then, because his telephone call to his superior did not occur until several minutes later, instead of immediately going to his office Murray likely continued to monitor the burning *Mont-Blanc* from the tug before he finally docked at Pier 9 around 9:00 a.m.

Murray reached his office and spoke by telephone to Rear-Admiral Chambers' deputy Captain James Turnbull at 9:04 a.m. Murray advised Turnbull a ship was

on fire in the Narrows, without reference to the ship's name, nationality—or dangerous cargo.

There is a simple explanation for this.

Mont-Blanc exploded before Murray could finish the conversation.

And in an instant the lives of sea transport officer Lieutenant James Murray and hundreds of others were snuffed out.

At the time of the explosion, paperwork for Murray's promotion had not yet been completed. He was posthumously promoted to lieutenant-commander.

THE HEROIC TELEGRAPH OPERATOR

On that fateful morning, Vincent Coleman and William Lovett were only 180 metres (200 yards) from Pier 6. Coleman's office controlled trains on the main line into Halifax, which ran along the western shore of Bedford Basin and through Rockingham Station to the passenger terminal at the North Street Station, located on the corner of Barrington and North Streets.

The No. 10 overnight express train from Saint John, New Brunswick, carrying nearly 300 passengers, was due to arrive at 8:55 a.m. Alerted by a sailor sent from *Hilford* by Murray, Lovett called CGR terminal agent Henry Dustan at 8:50 a.m. to warn him of a burning ship "loaded with explosives" heading for Pier 6.

After sending a warning message, Coleman and Lovett apparently left the CGR depot, but the dispatcher returned to the telegraph office and continued to send warning messages as far as Truro to stop trains inbound for Halifax.

But by then, it was too late.

The No. 10 had already passed Rockingham Station and could not be stopped, so his message had no effect on the train.

Coleman's heroism does not have to be embellished with invented "facts."

While his telegram may not have stopped the No. 10, it was certainly passed to Stewiacke, Shubenacadie and other railway telegraph stations along the mainline to Truro. This undoubtedly contributed to the early response of several communities outside of Halifax to the disaster.

"Hold up the train. Ammunition ship afire in harbour making for Pier 6 and will explode. Guess this will be my last message. Good-bye boys."

Popular version of Vincent Coleman's last Morse code message.

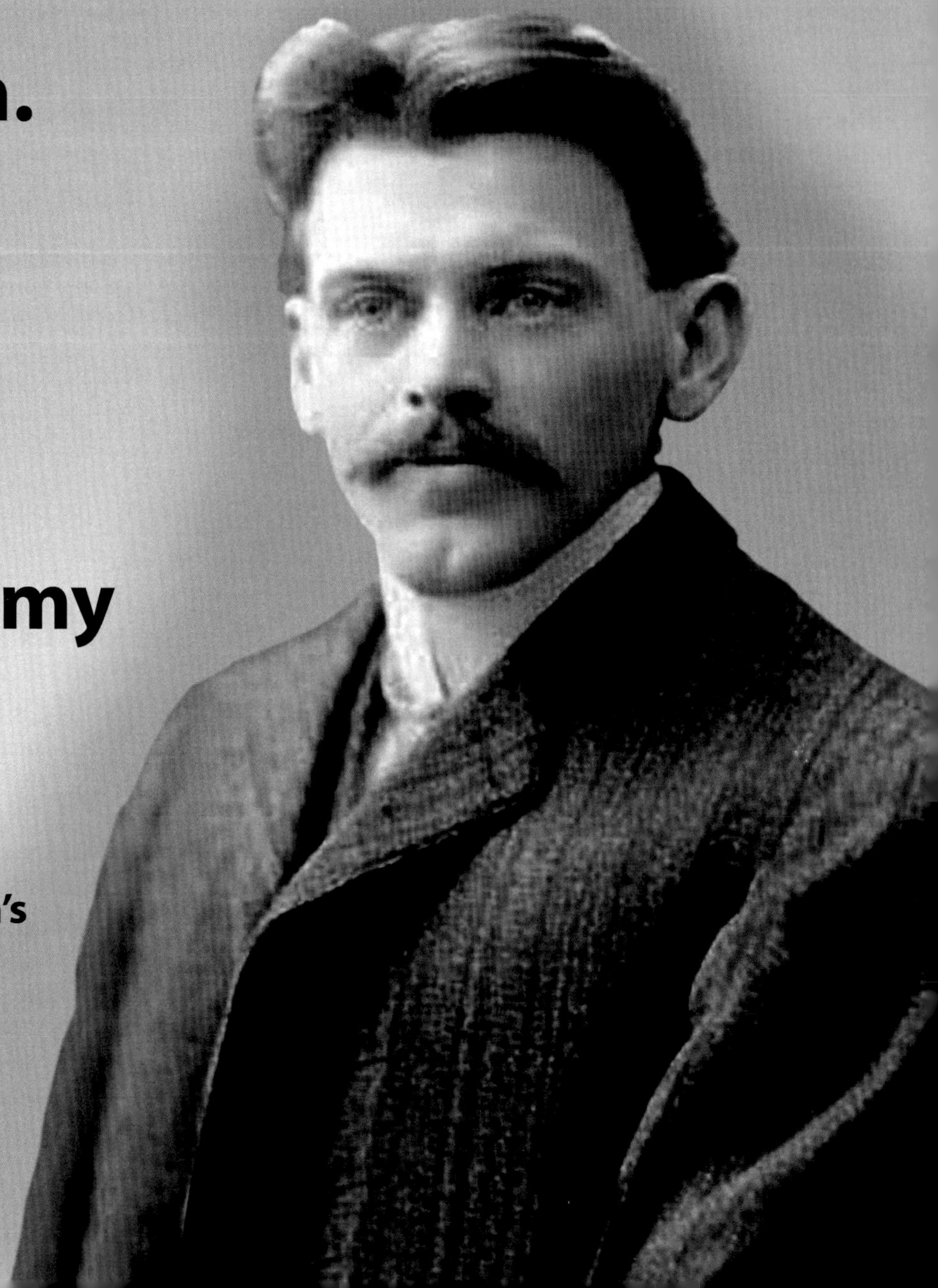

CHAPTER 4

DESCENT INTO HELL

A few workmen trudge along a rail line amid a scene of utter destruction.

DESTRUCTION

At 9:04:35 a.m., *Mont-Blanc* blew up.

The explosion tore through the ship and her cargo at speeds of approximately 7,600 metres (almost five miles) per second, created temperatures in excess of 3,000°C and vapourized the water surrounding the ship.

The vessel simply disappeared.

A massive, whitish-grey, billowing cloud shot more than 3,600 metres (11,800 feet) into the skies, dwarfing the smoke caused by the fire.

The explosion sent waves radiating outwards through earth, air and water from the spot where *Mont-Blanc* had been a millisecond earlier. A dramatic increase in temperature and air pressure caused the leading edge of the blast wave to expand outwards with concussive force at supersonic speed, followed immediately by a high-velocity shock wave.

The blast and shock waves destroyed everything in their path. As this supersonic wall of air expanded outwards, it left a partial vacuum behind it. The massive compression was followed by an equally massive and opposing decompression as air rushed in to fill the vacuum.

"All at once there was a most hideous noise & I saw the whole boat [*Mont-Blanc*] vanish...I was hurled on the deck and there was an awful noise going on...I ran along the deck & heard all kinds of things falling. It was shrapnel & bits of the side of the ship."

Able Seaman Bert Griffith, HMCS *Niobe*.

Some people who may have survived the initial blast did not withstand this second shock, as the maelstrom propelled deadly daggers of glass and wood, along with tonnes of other debris, back toward the harbour.

This phenomenon explains why some houses had their windows and doors blown outwards, or toppled trees pointed towards the harbour.

In an instant, large swaths of houses and other buildings along the harbour front and in the community of Richmond were obliterated.

Piers splintered and disappeared.

Small vessels disintegrated.

Large ships had their superstructures scoured away.

Wooden buildings shattered inwards or burst outwards.

Masonry buildings collapsed onto their foundations.

"The windows all came in, the inside walls collapsed and leaned against each other... There was a rain of chimney bricks, bits of steel, and worst of all, flying glass."

Cadet Harry Kingsley, Royal Naval College of Canada.

Wagons and trucks, trains and trams, cars and cranes were tossed into the air, bowled over and smashed against buildings, each other or various objects.

Trees and telegraph poles were uprooted or snapped in half like toothpicks.

Hundreds of thousands of loose objects of all sizes were swept up into the whirlwind and flew through the air to cause death, injury or damage.

Further away in the city, buildings shook, plaster cracked and windows shattered into thousands of deadly daggers.

A typical example of a house destroyed in the explosion: roof blown off, windows and doors shattered and walls imploded, among other damage.

FIRST VICTIMS

The fire engine *Patricia* was wrecked in the explosion but was rebuilt by its manufacturer, the La France Fire Engine Company.

The first victims were those closest to the burning vessel: crews of *Stella Maris*, *Highflyer* and *Niobe*, as well as the firemen in *Patricia* and Chief Condon's car, all of whom had come to *Mont-Blanc*'s immediate aid.

Aboard the tug, Second Mate Nickerson was just about to come up from below with the 10-inch hawser when *Mont-Blanc* exploded. Brannen and 18 of his 24-man crew were killed. The five injured survivors were below deck or shielded by the funnel, although two of them died of their injuries a few days later. Brannen's son and Nickerson survived.

Highflyer's whaler was lifted into the air and propelled towards the Dartmouth shore before crashing down onto the water. Only Able Seaman William Becker survived, although he nearly drowned before struggling ashore through icy water.

Mont-Blanc exploded as *Niobe*'s whaler pulled towards *Imo*, about 275 metres (300 yards) away. The force of the explosion blew *Niobe*'s pinnace and its crew to pieces.

On Pier 6, the fire chief and seven of his men, including his deputy, also died instantly when *Mont-Blanc* exploded. Another fireman succumbed to his injuries on New Year's Eve.

Patricia was a jumbled mass of wrecked machinery.

Miraculously, *Patricia*'s driver, Billy Wells, survived.

"The sight was awful, with people hanging out of windows dead. Some with their heads missing, and some thrown onto the overhead telegraph wires."

Firefighter Billy Wells.

The blast catapulted him from the driver's seat and the tsunami that followed knocked him unconscious. When he regained consciousness, he was far from Pier 6, wet and completely naked, with deep wounds in the muscles of his right arm. His left arm was uninjured, Bizarrely, it still gripped a piece of *Patricia*'s steering wheel.

Wells spent two days on a hospital floor waiting for a bed and a further five months in hospital recuperating.

Amazingly, the La France Fire Engine Company rebuilt *Patricia*. The company also presented Wells with the remaining piece of the steering wheel.

Although these seamen and fireman were the first to die, the time between their deaths and 1,600 others was imperceptible.

It only took half a second for the blast wave to reach its maximum destructive power.

Captain Le Médec, his crew and Pilot Mackey had barely made it inside the treeline on the Dartmouth side when their ship exploded. Although all were thrown to the ground and the captain and the pilot were knocked unconscious, they were alive. The most serious injury was the broken arm of a 20-year-old gunner. He died the next day, "having lost all his blood," according to Le Médec.

Those aboard *Imo* were not so fortunate. On the bridge, only the helmsman, John Johansen survived. Captain From, Chief Officer Iverson and Pilot Hayes were killed. Four other crew members also died. The deaths of From, Iverson and Hayes meant that much of *Imo*'s version of the events that led to the collision was unavailable.

(left): Ground Zero of the explosion, where Pier 6 stood formerly, now completely vanished. The broken wreck of *Stella Maris* lies close to shore.

(bottom): This clock, found in explosion ruins, had its hands frozen at the exact time of the blast.

SHOCK AND BLAST WAVES

"People with hardly any clothes on were running up and down the streets. Men were crying for their families and women were crying for children still trapped in the burning houses. Some were kneeling in the streets praying to God for help. It was a terrible sight."

Annie Chapman, survivor.

At the western edge of Richmond, the destructive wave hit Fort Needham Hill, dissipating some of its force upwards. Further south, Citadel Hill caused the same effect, but to a greater degree because of its larger size and greater distance from the explosion.

At the very northern tip of the peninsula along the shore of Bedford Basin, the historic black community of Africville was protected to a degree by the bluff of Richmond Hill above it. It endured extensive building damage similar to other locations near the devastated area, such as blown-in doors, shattered windows and collapsed roofs. Some of its residents suffered injuries and four of them were killed. Only one—eight-year-old Aldora Andrews—is positively known to have been in the community at the time. Her mother's arm was broken, while her father had back and leg injuries.

Hundreds of small fires broke out as stoves were tipped over, spilling hot coals or wooden embers onto floors, to be fed by wooden walls and ceilings that collapsed around them. As the fires spread, they found a new source of fuel in coal or cordwood stored in basements or sheds.

Choking smoke filled the air, carrying pungent smells of burning wood from hundreds of blazing houses.

Soon the unmistakeable sickly-sweet odour of burnt flesh was added to it.

Pieces of *Mont-Blanc* rained down as more than 2,700 tonnes (3,000 tons) of deadly, red-hot missiles, causing more death and injury. Black, sooty oil accompanied this falling cloud of shrapnel, which covered people and entered open wounds, staining skin.

Many injured survivors bore these indelible "explosion tattoos" for the rest of their lives.

The explosion scooped up boulders, rocks and stones from the exposed harbour bottom, which joined the hail of *Mont-Blanc* shrapnel and came crashing back to earth to kill, maim and damage.

They were everywhere—bodies and parts of bodies strewn throughout the devastated area.

Some were charred beyond recognition, others so horrifically disfigured or mutilated relatives never identified them.

The force of the blast killed many, some by being blown apart, while others died from flying objects the detonation hurled through the air, against or into their bodies.

Others drowned in the roaring tsunami that immediately followed the explosion.

Still others remained buried out of sight, crushed beneath the rubble of collapsed houses or buildings.

Perhaps the worse fate of all awaited those trapped alive amid burning debris, terrified and helplessly ensnared as searing flames licked toward them, their screams unheard.

Others lay trapped in wreckage that was not aflame, but who could not be pulled free before a severe blizzard began that night and continued through the next day, doomed to death by exposure.

In addition to human bodies, carcasses and parts of animals—dogs, cats, horses, cows, pigs and chickens—lay scattered grotesquely throughout the north end.

The air, earth and water waves did not stop at Halifax.

They caused church bells to ring in towns several kilometres away, while the infrasound (low-frequency sound near or below human hearing) of the explosion refracted back to earth was felt as far away as Cape Breton and Prince Edward Island.

TSUNAMI

Parts of Dartmouth suffered as much damage as north end Halifax, but the town's fate is often ignored in many accounts of the explosion.

In the harbour, the explosion roiled the water like a giant cauldron, sucked it away from the harbour bottom, exposed the seabed and sent a tsunami or tidal wave crashing outwards in a semicircle. The giant bore attacked shipping, tore large vessels from their moorings and sucked smaller craft into it.

Human and animal bodies—dead and alive—suffered the same fate.

Alan Ruffman and his associates have done extensive research on the tsunami. Their findings indicate the wave hit the Dartmouth shore opposite first at about 10 metres (33 feet) above sea level, swept inland as far as Windmill Road, oscillated back across the harbour and swept up the Halifax shore as far as the third cross street.

The tsunami carried bodies and debris up the shores with each oscillation, eventually to flush them into the harbour.

It lifted the tug *Hilford* out of the water and unceremoniously dumped her some nine metres (30 feet) on top of the debris that buried Pier 9.

The wave that headed northward squeezed through the Narrows at a height of more than 10 metres, entered Bedford Basin at four to six metres (13 to 20 feet) and raced across the basin at a height of about three metres (10 feet), to crash against its surrounding shores. It reached the head of the basin an estimated eight minutes after the explosion.

"I have never seen death in this form before. I am sure that for 10 minutes we have all been thru worse than in the trenches. The whole town is a wreck…"

Able Seaman Bert Griffith in a letter to his wife, December 8, 1917.

The wave that flooded down the harbour channel travelled the greatest distance. It left the southern end of the Narrows at about six metres (20 feet), smashed into Georges Island five minutes later at two metres (6.5 feet) height, flowed onto McNabs and Lawlor Islands, swept through the outer approaches and into the open Atlantic about 18 minutes later.

Reports of vessels many kilometres out to sea being hit by the tsunami are inaccurate.

In fact, they experienced the same infrasound as some locations a long distance from Halifax did.

According to some early reports, the tsunami killed an estimated 200 people, a figure repeated without question over the years. Based on more recent studies, Ruffman believes this figure is too high, although the exact number remains unknown.

Any bodies found in or near the harbour did not necessarily mean the tsunami killed them. Many bodies blown into the water by the explosion were already dead, some to be swept onto the shore by the tidal wave.

Curious Connection: The 1857 Explosion

Halifax had known a previous large explosion. Early on Friday, August 14, 1857, the Merchant's Powder Magazine in Halifax, containing four-and-a half tonnes (five tons) of gunpowder, mysteriously exploded. The last person to have access to the magazine—indeed the only person to have free access to the magazine—was its most frequent customer, Sandy Keith, aka "the Dynamite Fiend." Keith was acting as the agent of his uncle, the wealthy brewer Alexander Keith. Haligonian society refused to believe the perpetrator could be one of their own and Keith remained above overt suspicion.

The ground or seismic wave probably weakened some structures, but it caused minimal damage, as its magnitude was quite small. It did however, allow scientists to finally pinpoint the exact time of the explosion—65 years after it occurred.

Using calculations based on long-buried records of Dalhousie University's seismograph, Ruffman discovered the explosion occurred at 9:04:35, plus or minus ten seconds.

(top) This panorama view was taken from Pier 8 looking west toward Richmond, beyond the shattered rail cars.

(left): Booklets containing photographs of the disaster were a popular contemporary item.

THE COLEMAN FAMILY

Although historians continue to debate whether Coleman's initial message actually contributed to stopping the No. 10 train, other stations further along the line received the message before the connection with Halifax went dead.

Both Bill Lovett and Vince Coleman died as a result of the explosion—Coleman instantly and Lovett later in hospital.

At Coleman's house in Richmond his family felt the force of the explosion. Seven-year-old Eleanor Coleman was in the midst of morning prayers with her schoolmates at St. Joseph's School when she felt the building shake and heard a booming crash. As pieces of ceiling plaster fell on the terrified girls, the nun in charge of the class got them moving and out of the building—just before the ceiling collapsed.

Leaving the confusion in the schoolyard, Eleanor made her way home on streets littered with debris and lined with flaming rubble where houses once stood.

Thick smoke stung her eyes and burned her throat.

All about her, injured people screamed for help.

Some ran about aimlessly, while others dug frantically in the wreckage with bare, bleeding hands. Others—more severely injured—could only drag themselves along the streets.

When Eleanor got to the place where her house stood only a short while ago, she found it reduced to an unidentifiable mass of smoking debris.

Her brother and one of her sisters were already there, feverishly tossing broken boards and chunks of plaster aside in a mad search for their mother, Frances, and baby sister, Eileen.

The sound of the baby crying spurred their efforts and they dug faster.

Suddenly, they found Frances unconscious under part of a collapsed kitchen wall, with Eileen half a metre away, badly cut on her neck where the kitchen sink had crashed down on her.

As flames drew nearer, the three children lifted their mother and baby sister from the rubble. They then made their way to Gottingen Street through thick smoke and dangerously close flames.

When Frances revived, she was lying on a cold sidewalk on Gottingen Street, a stabbing pain in her back.

She looked about in bewilderment. What had happened—and where was her husband, Vince?

Frances discovered the sad truth a short time later, when searchers found her husband's body in the shattered wreckage of what had been his dispatcher's shed.

Railway officials later presented her with Vince's telegraph key, pen and watch.

(above left): Baby Eileen Coleman's bloodstained dress has been preserved in the Maritime Museum of the Atlantic.

(above right): A number of Vincent Coleman's personal belongings—plus his telegraph key—were presented to his wife, Frances, by railroad authorities.

Personality Profile: Patrick Vincent Coleman

Patrick Vincent Coleman, 45, was a telegraph operator and train dispatcher for the CGR, formerly known as the Intercolonial Railway of Canada. Rightly or wrongly, he is recognized today as one of the heroes of the disaster. Coleman was interred in Mount Olivet Roman Catholic Cemetery in Halifax and was survived by his wife Frances, who lived until 1970. A street is named after him in Clayton Park, in 2007 a section of Albert Street near his old home was renamed Vincent Street and in 2017 one of two new harbour ferries was named in his honour. He was inducted into the Canadian Railway Hall of Fame in 2004. A condominium that overlooks the mass burial site of a number of unidentified explosion victims is named The Vincent Coleman.

TURTLE GROVE

A small Mi'kmaq settlement had existed on the Dartmouth side of the harbour along the shores of Tuft's Cove for many years.

For several decades, a small Mi'kmaq community known as Turtle Grove stood on the shores of Tuft's Cove, a tiny inlet on the Dartmouth side of the harbour, where the water squeezes through the Narrows. It is not known precisely when the Mi'kmaq established permanent residence at Turtle Grove, but the community certainly dated as far back as the late 1700s.

The small settlement—a few families on four-and-a-half hectares (11 acres) of rocky land with 150 metres (500 feet) of waterfront—nestled north of the Oland Brewery, close to the North End Ferry. They eked out a living as best they could, living in wigwams in the summer and rough wooden huts during the winter.

As Dominion officials did not recognize the settlement as a reserve, it received little government assistance. But by November 1917, lobbying by the Mi'kmaq and sympathetic Indian agents paid off and the government agreed to establish a reserve for the Turtle Grove Mi'kmaq. There was just one slight catch; the reserve would not be on the harbour, but a few kilometres away, near Albro Lake in Dartmouth.

As the residents contemplated their forthcoming move, *Mont-Blanc* collided with *Imo* and the people in Turtle Grove rushed to the shoreline to watch the flaming spectacle. When *Mont-Blanc* blew up, the small settlement, like the Halifax shore opposite, took the full brunt of the explosion and was completely destroyed.

Of the 12 men, women and children known to have died at Turtle Grove, survivors recovered nine bodies. More may have died among the 24 confirmed residents, but the total number remains unknown because no authorities kept records of the inhabitants.

Although little was written about Turtle Grove, some contemporary newspapers recorded the complete destruction of the Mi'kmaq community. One of the few accounts tells of "the closing scene of Indian life in Dartmouth," with the "remnant" of Turtle Grove's population "pitifully making their way to Town, carrying their dead and injured."

Most survivors of the explosion left Turtle Grove, although five remained. Eventually, they either died or left, and a small Mi'kmaq community that was virtually unknown to most city residents disappeared forever. Tonnes of fill covered the last vestiges of the historic Mi'kmaq settlement on the shores of *Kjipuktuk* in 1965. Nova Scotia Light and Power (now Nova Scotia Power) constructed a generating station on the site, which today features three 157-metre (515-foot) tall smokestacks, known locally as the "Three Sisters."

“The old time Indian wail could be heard for over a mile. It was a never-to-be-forgotten sight.”

Halifax newspaper, 1919.

A Mi’kmaq group in ceremonial dress of the late nineteenth and early twentieth centuries, probably taken between 1890 and 1895.

A rare photograph of *Middleham Castle*, her funnel bent by the force of the explosion.

Although the explosion affected members of many families—including extended families—the family of north end residents James and Elizabeth Jackson suffered the most loss. James and two other family members had died before the explosion, leaving some 74 souls still living: Elizabeth, five sons and four daughters plus their spouses, 48 grandchildren and five great grandchildren. Eight members of the family were away from Richmond on the day, leaving 66 in the community.

By 9:10 on the morning of December 6, 48 of them were dead, all within a three-block area.

The remaining 18 were injured.

Within the Jackson clan, a daughter, Mary, and her husband Joseph Hinch, sustained the largest loss of life for a single family. Only Mary survived, although she sustained severe injuries and remained trapped under debris for 24 hours.

Her husband and all 10 of their children died.

So much death and injury inflicted on one family within five minutes is hard to fathom.

Other extended families had several of their members killed, but none equalled the tragedy wrought upon the Jacksons.

Many young children performed heroic acts in the minutes following the explosion:

- Norman Roberts, age eight, rescued his mother and baby sister from their burning house.
- Pearl Hartlen, nine, tried to drag her unconscious mother from the ruins of their home, but her mother's skirt caught on the debris. With nothing to cut it, Pearl bit and tore at the fabric until she could pull her mother to safety.
- Cecilia McGrath, 11, led eight other girls safely out of the ruins of a school.
- Agnes Foran, 12, rescued her mother and baby brother, despite having a large piece of glass embedded in her stomach.
- Roland Theakson, 14, directed 35 small school boys to exit their damaged school according to the fire drill they had practiced.

The force of the earth, air and water waves dissipated rapidly as they flowed outwards.

Blessed silence descended momentarily on Halifax and Dartmouth.

Then screams of pain and pitiful cries for help began to fill the air.

Incredible Incidents: Flying Through the Air

Among the strangest of all experiences undergone by survivors of the explosion were those who literally "flew through the air." Some were flung great distances and had injuries, while others escaped with minor or no injuries. Among them:

-Charles John Mayers, 22, third officer on the British freighter *Middleham Castle*, was lifted from the deck of his ship by the blast and thrown to the top of Needham Hill, 800 metres (0.5 miles) away. As he flew through the air "quite conscious," he remembered a "revolving sensation, meeting pieces of timber and wood" and feeling wet as he came down. The landing knocked him out; when he awoke, he was badly cut and picked "nails and pieces of wood" from his face. He was naked except for his boots.

-Barbara Orr, 14, experienced the same phenomenon. She was running downhill across Mulgrave Park when Mont-Blanc exploded. When she regained consciousness, she was lying on top of Needham Hill, about 800 metres away. She remembered having a sensation of moving violently, "thinking that I was going down deep holes all the time." One foot was smashed and she was cut, bruised, bleeding and covered with oil and soot. Like many other survivors, Barbara was left with a permanent black mark –this one on the side of her face.

"There was a little girl near me and I asked her where we were. She was crying and said she did not know where we were."

Charles Mayers, recollection of meeting Barbara Orr on top of Needham Hill.

Fact Sheet: Naval Heroes

Many city residents blamed the fledgling RCN for the Halifax Explosion, believing it failed to adequately control shipping in the harbour. Yet, at the individual level, several sailors—Canadian and British—performed acts of heroism immediately before and after the devastating explosion.

For their actions that morning, the crew of *Niobe*'s pinnace received posthumous awards. Acting Boatswain Mattison and Stoker Petty Officer Beard received the Albert Medal in Bronze, while the five other sailors with them received letters of appreciation.

Similarly, some of the crew of *Highflyer*'s whaler received posthumous awards. Acting Commander Triggs received the Albert Medal in Gold (at right), while Becker—the lone survivor aboard the whaler—received the Albert Medal in Bronze.

"The boat's crew were fully aware of the desperate nature of the work they were engaged on, and by their gallantry and devotion to duty they sacrificed their lives in the endeavour to save the lives of others."

From the Albert Medal in Bronze citation for Acting Boatswain Albert Mattison and Stoker Petty Officer Edward Beard, HMCS *Niobe*.

The explosion also set afire the ocean-going tug *Musquash*, which carried ammunition. *High Flyer*'s captain asked another tug to take *Musquash* in tow, but the crew were unwilling to board the disabled vessel. Two British sailors, Leading Seaman Thomas Davis and Able Seaman Robert Stones, volunteered to board *Musquash*, now broken loose from her moorings. They secured a line and the tug towed *Musquash* into the middle of the harbour. Then they went forward, pulled the ammunition—by now badly scorched—away from the flames and threw it overboard.

The tender *W.H. Lee* arrived and Davis and Stones broke down doors to allow *Lee's* fire hoses to put out the fire. The sailors' actions subdued the fire and prevented further damage and loss of life, as the ammunition could have exploded at any time. For their heroic acts, Davis and Stones also received the Albert Medal in Bronze.

While the disaster unfolded in the harbour, two navy divers from *Niobe* were working underwater off the Dockyard pier. Four men manned the hand-operated air pumps, while another two paid out the divers' line under the watchful eye of Chief Master-at-Arms John Gammon. When *Mont-Blanc* blew up, one diver was in the water while the other descended a ladder. The explosion killed five of the six sailors on the wharf, but both divers and Gammon survived.

The surviving sailor, Able Seaman Walter Critch, realized he had to get air to the divers immediately. Although the pump remained undamaged, the pump house roof had collapsed onto it. Critch could not clear the fallen roof, so he squeezed in between it and the pump and gave a mighty heave upwards with his shoulders.

He moved bits of wreckage off the pump wheels, held up the collapsed roof with one hand and started the pump with the other. The piston slowly began to suck in air. It usually took four men to operate the pump, but somehow Critch managed single-handedly to start a trickle of air going to the divers. At the same time, Gammon rushed to the ladder to get the divers up and their face masks open.

For their quick actions, Critch received the Meritorious Service Medal (Naval), while Gammon was made a Member of the Order of the British Empire.

The Albert Medal

The Albert Medal was instituted in 1866 in memory of Prince Albert, Queen Victoria's husband, in two classes. It was awarded to those who, "in saving or endeavouring to save the lives of others from shipwreck or other peril of the sea, endangered their own lives." In 1877 awards of the medal were extended to saving life on land.

The Hour of Horror in Devastated Richmond by future Group of Seven artist Arthur Lismer. From 1916 to 1919 he was principal of the city's Victoria School of Art and Design, now the Nova Scotia College of Art and Design.

CHAPTER 5

FIRST RESPONSES

INITIAL REACTIONS

Within seconds of the explosion, some of the surviving residents of Halifax and Dartmouth instinctively began the grim task of helping the injured—and recovering the dead—from homes, work places and other buildings.

Others slipped into a catatonic stupor, frozen by the enormity of what had just happened.

Initial rescue attempts were unorganized. Pockets of bleeding and dazed survivors throughout the devastated area spontaneously started to dig through the rubble—many with their bare hands.

In particular, family members who survived the explosion began a frantic search for their loved ones in the giant jigsaw jumble of burning, smoking ruins. Other relatives outside the devastated zone at the time—mostly men at their workplaces—attempted to return to their homes and families as quickly as possible.

This task was made much more difficult as widespread destruction had wiped out many landmarks and covered streets in debris, making it difficult to know exactly where one was.

"Around was confusion beyond description. The stacks of timber, the debris of the piers and railway sheds, the ties and lines of the sidings which had been torn up by the wave were inextricably mixed up and piled in heaps, which I can only compare to a box of spillikin [a game similar to pick-up sticks] on a gigantic scale."

Rear-Admiral Bertram Chambers, Port Convoy Officer.

Soldiers search through debris for victims of the disaster. Instant military assistance after the explosion was instrumental in recovery operations.

Members of the Halifax Police Department pose on the steps of the Grand Parade, July 1914.

POLICE AND FIREMEN

Sadly, with hundreds of small fires burning uncontrollably throughout the north end, there were too few able-bodied people immediately available to help the many victims trapped in the wreckage of their homes or other structures.

As a result, several succumbed to the horrible death of being slowly burned alive before they could be freed.

Additionally, Halifax—like other Canadian cities of its size at the time—was ill-equipped municipally to handle a disaster the magnitude and scope of the explosion.

The police force consisted of 39 men: Chief Frank Hanrahan, one detective, eight sergeants and 29 constables. In addition, the department had recently hired eight temporary men to help deal with increased crime caused by the war.

After the explosion, 32 permanent and 120 volunteer firefighters remained to confront an impossible job. They possessed seven steam engines, two chemical engines, eight hose wagons and four ladder trucks—all horse-drawn—to assist them.

Additional equipment and firemen from across the province started to arrive by train later that day. Unfortunately, most of their hoses proved useless as their threads were not standardized with Halifax's.

As well, there were no establishments such as today's public safety or emergency measures organizations to take charge in a disaster and coordinate an orderly, timely response.

HOSPITALS

Halifax had a number of public, military and private hospitals (publicly-funded universal health care did not exist at the time). Together, they contained perhaps a thousand beds. In the end, hospitals treated about 4,000 victims (and private doctors saw many hundreds more), while about 2,500 required hospitalization. One of the military hospitals—the Pier 2 casualty clearing station—had been destroyed in the blast.

"Camp Hill [military hospital] will almost be a synonym for horror...The sights were terrible...broken bones, scalds, burns due to the contact with stoves or boilers, contusions, maiming, internal injuries—but undoubtedly the most ghastly wounds were those inflicted by the flying glass. Heads and faces, bodies, limbs, were rent and gashed in all conceivable ways. Huge pieces of flesh were gouged out by glass."

Archibald MacMechan, Director, Halifax Disaster Record Office.

Soon all these hospitals—and several instant makeshift ones—overflowed with a jumble of confused and injured humanity. At the height of the relief efforts, more than 40 hospitals were in operation, many of them fully or partially staffed by military personnel.

In the first hours before outside help arrived, overworked medical staff laboured to the point of exhaustion—and beyond.

When certain anaesthetics ran out, doctors performed operations without them.

Some victims died before medical staff could get to them.

And for many of those who survived the explosion but were physically or psychologically scarred, recuperation became a lifelong undertaking.

Dartmouth also had a hospital, but it did not treat physically injured or ill patients. The Nova Scotia Hospital was the province's psychiatric facility. Despite its purpose, a steady stream of injured and homeless residents made their way to the hospital throughout the day. The single doctor on duty and the nursing staff coped as best they could until finally augmented by nine additional doctors that evening.

Canadian army medical orderlies stand outside of St. Mary's College on Windsor Street, which was turned into a 150-bed hospital by the Boston Red Cross Hospital Unit.

(opposite top): Patients and army nursing sisters pose in a makeshift hospital set up in a gymnasium after the explosion.

(opposite bottom): *Fearing a Second Explosion* by Arthur Lismer depicts survivors on their panicked journey away from the ammunition magazine in Wellington Barracks.

FALSE ALARM

Many public and private facilities in both communities became emergency hospitals to handle large numbers of the injured. Among them were a 150-bed one at the YMCA on Barrington Street and a 70-bed one at the Waegwoltic Club on the Northwest Arm. In Dartmouth, large private homes and a school also became temporary hospitals.

The Red Cross, Victorian Order of Nurses and St. John's Ambulance Brigade provided minor medical assistance, both in homes throughout the devastated area, as well as in the emergency dressing stations established throughout the area.

In 1917, various social services provided by governments today were largely non-existent. Private organizations filled that role, including the Charitable Irish Association, the Halifax Association for Improving the Conditions of the Poor, the Salvation Army and a number of churches and other groups.

All of these organizations quickly responded to the disaster and were sorely tested in the days following the explosion.

"Men, women and children of all sorts and classes were literally packed in the ward like sardines in a box, the cots all occupied, and the floors covered so that it was difficult to step between them."

Dr. W.B. Moore, Kentville.

Critical rescue operations were needlessly interrupted around mid-morning when an unfounded rumour spread that the garrison wooden ammunition magazine inside Wellington Barracks (the northern part of today's CFB Stadacona) was on fire and in danger of exploding. People saw smoke rising from the magazine, but it was actually a cloud of steam caused when an officer sprayed a fire extinguisher on hot coals from a nearby overturned hot water heater.

The hubbub around the magazine instantly alarmed a nearby crowd of survivors on Campbell Road (now Barrington Street).

Someone yelled, "The magazine was on fire."

Word quickly circulated among both civilians and soldiers that an evacuation of the north end had been ordered.

The general panic at the thought of a second explosion took on a life of its own. Soon long lines of survivors, many injured and most blackened with soot, made their way southwards toward the protection offered by the open spaces of the Common, the stout walls of the Citadel or the distance of Point Pleasant Park.

The general movement southward clogged city streets and slowed vehicles and wagons moving northward with help or acting as ambulances. It is difficult to say how many additional people died as a result of this panicky rumour, but undoubtedly many individuals who had survived the explosion, but remained trapped, died as fires consumed them.

Others died on their journey south even as new life entered the world, hastened by the shock of the explosion.

The end result was the loss of approximately two hours of time that could have been better spent saving victims stuck helplessly in the burning ruins—along with many of their lives.

Despite the evacuation panic, several brave souls chose to ignore it and remained in the north end, where they continued to fight fires, rescue victims, administer first aid and provide what comfort they could.

"No one shall leave this building. It would mean the death of many of the children if they had to be moved... and it is the duty of everyone to stand by our post, and if it should be that we are to die, we will die at our post."

Superintendent, Children's Hospital.

IMMEDIATE RELIEF

At the time, speedy methods of civilian long-distance communications facilities in and out of Halifax consisted of telegraph and telephone using land lines.

The military possessed a wireless radio capability, and although civilian wireless telegraphy and radio existed, they were in their infancy and hampered by wartime restrictions.

With telephone and telegraph connections destroyed or damaged in the explosion, and the military wireless capability temporarily incapacitated as essential antennas had been knocked down, it took some time to get out word of the scope of the disaster.

The initial, unorganized rescue initiatives were quickly superseded by systematic rescue and recovery efforts. There was one reason why these secondary efforts were established so quickly: the huge army and naval presence in Halifax.

Major-General Thomas Benson, General Officer Commander Military District 6 (Nova Scotia), had immediately offered his troops to the civilian authorities for any assistance they could provide, a proposal quickly accepted.

Quite simply, if it were not for more than 5,000 Canadian and British soldiers and a large number of Canadian, British and American sailors in the city, more people would have died, more property damage would have occurred and quite possibly a degree of anarchy might have prevailed.

Soldiers prepare for land warfare their entire uniformed life, and the monumental battles of the First World War gave added impetus to this training.

The destruction wrought on Halifax was in every way comparable to the devastation the war brought to European communities in war zones.

Soldiers and sailors—assisted by surviving policemen, firefighters and others—dug through the rubble, searching for survivors; administered first aid; took victims to hospitals or other medical facilities; and delivered food, clothing and blankets as well as hundreds of other items, including supplies to board up blown-out windows and doors; and guarded against looters.

"I have never seen anything on the battlefront equal to the scenes of destruction that I witnessed in Halifax today."

Lieutenant-Colonel Frank McKelvey Bell, assistant director of medical services, Military District 6.

The first group of recruits from Nova Scotia for HMCS *Niobe* pose stiffly in their new uniforms. Sailors like these helped prevent further loss of life and destruction after the explosion.

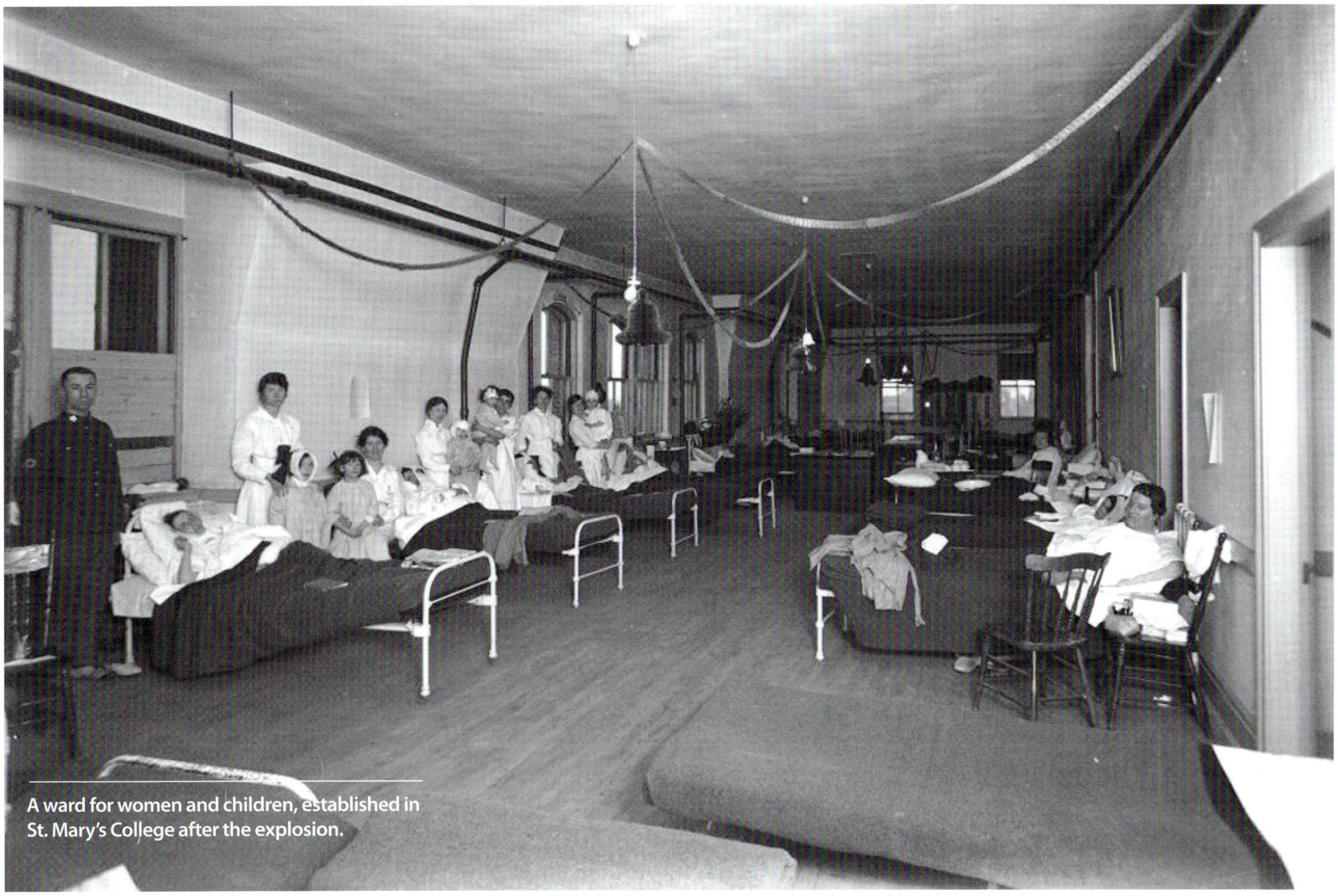

A ward for women and children, established in St. Mary's College after the explosion.

Owners of serviceable cars, trucks and horse-drawn wagons showed up spontaneously or were asked to transport victims to medical facilities.

If they did not volunteer, their vehicles were forcibly confiscated.

Among the 5,000 soldiers were 600 medical personnel along with military treatment facilities throughout the city, all of which were a godsend when it came to coping with the wide range and number of injured citizens.

Remarkably—with the possible exception of the first day—due to the large number of army and navy medical personnel already in Halifax, plus the speedy influx of doctors and nurses from the outside, there was never a shortage of medical staff.

Halifax's role as the Canadian city most involved in the war effort—a function that led to the explosion in the first place—was also the main reason why the reaction to the disaster was so quick and coordinated.

The important role the army played in the rescue and recovery operations has never been fully and formally recognized, not on the Halifax municipal website, at annual memorial services or elsewhere. Although many residents displayed a long-standing ill-will towards the navy, which they blamed for the explosion in the first place, no such accusations were ever leveled against the army.

It is a mystery why the contributions of the soldiers who offered so much in the explosion's aftermath have never been officially acknowledged, surely a bizarre oversight that has continued far too long.

"Urgent. Is there any possible way in which Militia Council can assist?"

Telegram from Major-General Willoughby Gwatkin, Chief of the General Staff, Ottawa

"Many thanks. Situation well in hand. Full report later."

Telegram reply from Major-General Benson, Commander Military District 6

NAVAL ASSISTANCE

Immediate help also came from several Canadian, British and American warships and merchant vessels at anchor in Halifax Harbour.

HM Ships *Highflyer* and *Changuinola*, US Coast Guard cutter *Morrill* and USS *Old Colony* immediately sent sailors ashore to assist. They systematically combed the wreckage for survivors, set up temporary first aid stations and transported the injured to hospitals or the larger British and American vessels with medical facilities.

Rescuers took many of the injured from other ships and along the waterfront to *Old Colony*, which, although not a hospital ship, was quickly converted into one by members of the Canadian Army Medical Corps.

The US Navy cruisers *Tacoma* and *Von Steuben* were nearby in the North Atlantic and saw the cloud from the explosion. Not knowing what to expect, they immediately changed course, headed for the wrecked city and arrived by early afternoon.

"They [troops stationed in Halifax] worked day and night to do all that was possible to assist all concerned in this terrible disaster."

Major-General Thomas Benson, Commander Military District 6.

At the request of General Benson, one of the first tasks of their crews was to patrol the downtown business district overnight to prevent looting from smashed store-fronts and give tired Canadian soldiers on duty all day an opportunity to rest.

By 8 p.m. soldiers had erected 400 tents equipped with wooden floors, cots, blankets, light and heat on the Common in front of the Armouries to see to the immediate needs of the homeless or those without adequate shelter, plus a 250-bed emergency marquee hospital. The tents were barely used however, partly due to a snowstorm the next day, but also because most civilians did not believe a tent could provide adequate shelter.

Neighbouring military districts also sent 34 medical officers and 54 nursing sisters, as well as additional medical and other supplies.

The USS *Old Colony* was in Halifax at the time and was quickly converted into a hospital ship by personnel of the Canadian Army Medical Corps.

Soldiers erected tents on the Common for the homeless, but most people were reluctant to use them.

Relief Committees

Initially, on December 6, the Relief Committee established an executive committee and five sub-committees: transportation, food, emergency shelter (which also established a number of first aid dressing stations), mortuary and finance. Further subcommittees followed:

- December 7: clothing, medical relief and fuel.
- December 8: managing, registration, medical supply, general supply and reconstruction.
- December 12: rehabilitation.

On December 7, Dartmouth formed its own Relief Committee, with a dozen sub-committees, many the same as in Halifax. It did have a few unique ones however, such as patrol, dumb animals and salvage.

HALIFAX RELIEF COMMITTEE

Within 45 minutes, officials formed the Halifax Relief Committee to manage all aspects of the crisis, in what surely must be a record for speedy action in the face of such an overwhelming disaster.

Around 11:30 that morning—while panic-stricken residents streamed from the north end—a number of Halifax's elected officials, bureaucrats, prominent citizens and ordinary people gathered at city hall to discuss relief efforts.

Lieutenant-Governor MacCallum Grant chaired the meeting. As Mayor Peter Martin was away, the senior city representative was Deputy Mayor Henry Colwell.

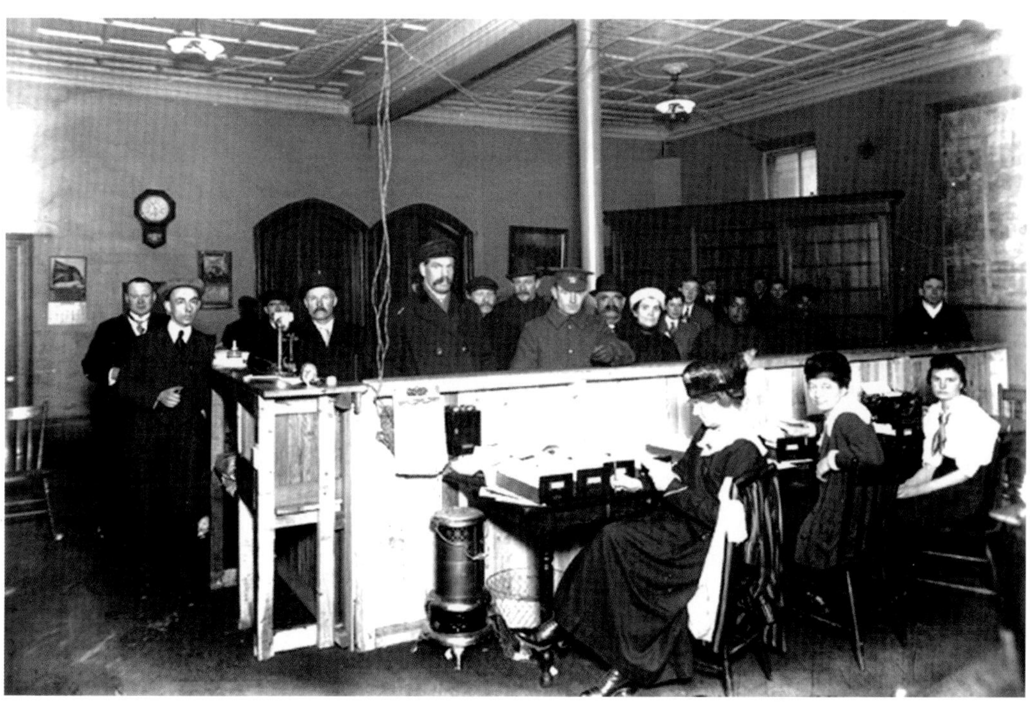

(above): Because Halifax Mayor Peter Martin was away from the city on December 6, his deputy, Henry Colwell, became the senior city member of the Relief Committee.

(left): Information, Registration and Employment Bureaus were set up in St. Mary's Army and Navy Club in St. Mary's Parish Hall on Barrington Street.

AMERICAN AID

After the explosion, messages sent by railway officials passed word of the disaster to the rest of Canada. One of the first people to do so was W.A. Duff, assistant chief engineer of the CGR. After viewing damage to the North Street Station and further north, he went to Rockingham and cabled Moncton, described the damage and requested help. Later the mayor asked him to relay similar messages to other towns.

George Graham, president of the Dominion Atlantic Railway, had already sent similar messages. Graham was in his private rail car in the railyard eating his breakfast when the explosion occurred. Unable to send any telegrams due to downed wires, he walked to the Rockingham Station to send requests for help to the outside world.

The railway quickly mobilized aid and sent a dozen relief trains with vital medical and other supplies, plus doctors, nurses and firefighters from towns across Nova Scotia and New Brunswick on the day of the disaster. Two days later help from other parts of Canada and the United States began to arrive.

Once trains deposited their personnel and supplies, many returned to their home locations carrying the injured, the homeless, orphaned children and others.

One of the most generous responses came from Boston, Massachusetts, a city and state linked closely to Halifax and Nova Scotia by many years of close personal and business ties. Massachusetts and the American Red Cross quickly established a relief committee. It organized a train with 11 doctors, 10 nurses and six representatives of relief agencies. The train left Boston at 10 p.m. that night, but due to snowstorms it did not arrive in Halifax until the afternoon of December 8. The Massachusetts expedition set up in Bellevue House, a mansion on Spring Garden Road used as an officers' mess, located where the Halifax Central Library now stands.

Another Massachusetts relief train arrived on December 9. It carried the Boston Red Cross Hospital Unit with 22 doctors and 69 nurses, along with sufficient supplies for a field hospital. They established a 150-bed hospital at St. Mary's College on Windsor Street.

Massachusetts also sent five social workers who provided invaluable assistance to the rehabilitation committee in getting discharged patients and the homeless into adequate shelter and ensuring follow up care.

Additional American medical contingents continued to arrive.

The State of Maine Hospital Unit came next. It took over the Ladies' College on Barrington Street and turned it into a 200-bed hospital, operated by 12 doctors and 13 nurses.

By the time 50 doctors and 52 nurses arrived from the Rhode Island Chapter of the American Red Cross on December 10, all medical facilities were fully staffed, so they canvassed door-to-door in the worst hit areas to treat any injured still in their homes.

Even staff from a private Boston hospital came to Halifax's aid. Its 10 doctors and four nurses set up in the YMCA. When another two doctors and nine nurses from the Maine Red Cross arrived, they were sent to various emergency dressing stations.

American medical relief workers pose in front of their train on arrival in Halifax.

The relief ships *Calvin Austin* and *Northland* also docked with additional aid from Boston: clothing, food, glass, building materials and 10 new trucks, along with 10 drivers and 10 drums of gasoline.

Another relief train departed New York City within hours of disaster. It carried cots, clothing, blankets, medical supplies and food, plus additional doctors and nurses.

In total, 222 doctors and 459 nurses from outside the city came to Halifax's aid.

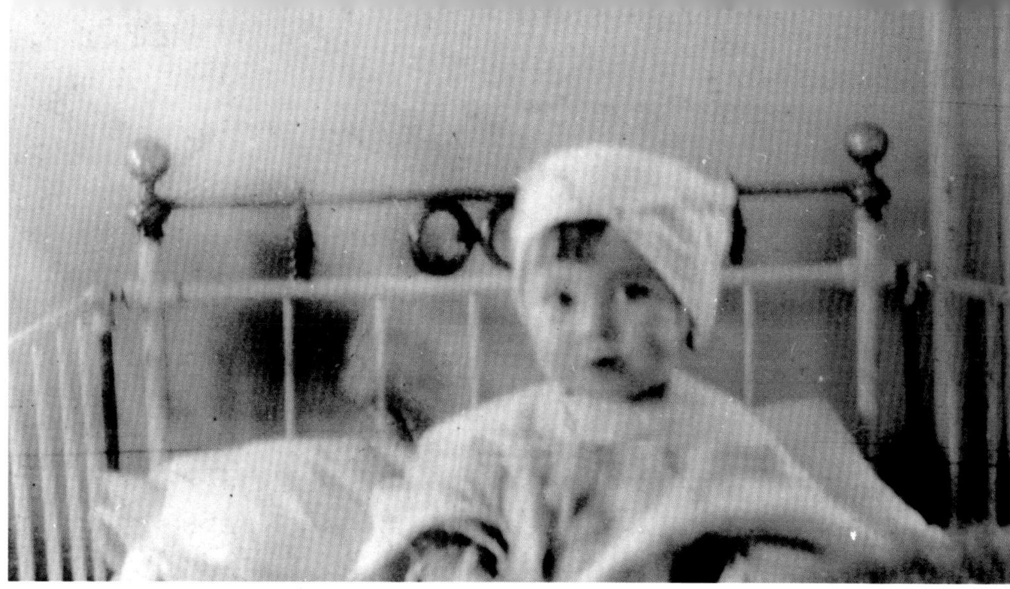

Incredible Incident: Ashpan Annie

Anne Liggins was almost 23 months old when the Halifax Explosion occurred. The blast levelled most of her family's home at 1414 Barrington Street in the city's north end and killed her mother, Anne, and brother, Edwin, age four. Her father, Edward, was a private serving overseas at the time. The explosion blew Anne under the kitchen stove, where the warm ashes in the ashpan kept her alive until she was found 26 hours later—suffering from only minor injuries and burns—by Sergeant-Major Davies, his dog and a neighbour, Benjamin Henneberry, who was searching for his own family nearby. Anne was taken to the Pine Hill Convalescent Hospital, where her grandmother and an aunt discovered her. Later, she worked in a laundry, married and raised a family. Her husband, Angus "Ginger" Welsh, died in the 1990s, while Anne passed away in 2010 in her room at The Berkeley seniors' residence at the age of 95. She is buried in Mount Olivet Roman Catholic Cemetery.

BLIZZARD

The story of 23-month-old Annie Liggins miraculous survival and subsequent rescue continues to amaze people.

By dawn on December 7, authorities were slowly getting control of the situation and a return to at least a modicum of normalcy was being effected.

Various relief committees had been organized, rescuers systematically combed the wreckage for more injured residents, firefighters brought fires under control, medical staff treated the injured, temporary accommodation had been secured for the homeless and the dead were being collected.

Then nature interfered to bring more misery and suffering to the battered communities.

Just before noon, snow began to fall, quickly developing into a raging snowstorm that hindered rescue, recovery and relief efforts. It continued all through December 8 and dumped more than 40 centimetres (16 inches) on the area.

Residents who remained in their battered houses, with only blankets or other flimsy coverings over blown-out windows and doors, now faced the grim prospect of freezing to death.

The new priority was to deliver food, warm clothing and heating fuel to homes, hospitals and shelters throughout the city. Volunteers struggled through deep snow drifts to get these essential supplies to those who needed them.

Despite these gallant efforts, several more people froze to death, trapped beneath rubble and debris.

On December 9, the weather turned, the snow melted and black slush flowed down gutters and hillsides.

But the respite—such as it was—was short-lived. More snow fell, temperatures dropped and layers of ice coated the ruined landscape.

"The peculiar blackness of the whole devastated area lighted by lurid jets of flame springing from the crater-like cellars of the ruins, with the fantastic shapes of those around destroyed homes, searching and probing vainly for their lost ones, and springing back from the shooting flames...and the blackened tree trunks in the region standing gaunt and spectral...with the rows of blackened and often half naked and twisted bodies of the dead...made a weird and desolate spectacle..."

Dr. W.B. Moore, Kentville.

"A team of horses was caught in the full blast of the explosion and probably killed outright through suffocation, yet they were partly erect and covered with a sheathing of ice so that the horses looked like a piece of statuary."

J. Prentice Murphy, secretary, Children's Aid Society, Boston Relief Expedition.

The snow inevitably slowed down rescue operations and led to additional deaths.

But thousands of dedicated men and women persevered under the most trying conditions in their attempts to find survivors, render aid to the rescued, arrange warm accommodation—and continue the grim search for bodies.

OVERCOMING ADVERSITY

One of the more amazing stories of someone blinded by the explosion is that of John "Eric" Davidson.

Davidson was two-and-a-half years old at the time. He was in his living room, along with his mother and sister, playing with a toy train on the window sill. He was facing the window when the explosion occurred and the shattered glass blinded him completely. Davidson attended the Halifax School for the Blind, where he studied music, but was much more interested in motor mechanics.

While his brothers read him instructions from auto repair manuals, he practiced on old cars in his family's back yard, using touch and memory to guide him. After an apprenticeship with a local car dealership, Davidson earned his motor mechanic's licence and worked for the city of Halifax as a mechanic until he retired in 1980.

But his true love was fiddling with old cars. Davidson was a founding member of a local antique car club and restored several classics. Although he was not supposed to, he would drive if given the chance, with someone telling him when to brake and turn.

He relished the sound of the engine and the wind in his hair while being driven or driving these old vehicles.

He also danced, learned to play the piano and banjo, did repairs around the house and went to bowling nights at United Memorial Church. In later life, Davidson moved to Berwick in the Annapolis Valley and lived there until he died in 2009, aged 94.

Blinded

For some reason, one of the injuries grossly exaggerated over the years is partial or total blindness. Frequently, figures of more than 1,000 people losing sight in one or both eyes are reported, equating to one in every 70 residents of Halifax at the time.

The actual numbers were considerably less.

Hundreds of explosion survivors did suffer eye injuries, the result of standing behind windows watching the burning *Mont-Blanc* when she exploded. Officials initially thought as many as 500 people might have been permanently blinded. A report prepared in January 1918 by the American Red Cross unit at Halifax however, counted the final number of all types of eye injuries as 691. A Victorian Order of Nurses survey conducted three months later matched this number exactly.

These results included 41 totally blinded and 260 with one eye blinded, plus another 170 classed as one or both eyes doubtful.

This discrepancy is partially explained by the fact that within a few days after the explosion, it became clear many of those who initially reported eye injuries actually retained their vision in one or both eyes once inflammation and irritation went away.

In the end, doctors treated 592 people with eye injuries. They performed 249 enucleations (eye removals), of which 16 were double enucleations.

At the time, Nova Scotia was a North American leader in dealing with blind people. The Halifax School for the Blind opened in 1867 and in 1882 the province passed an act to ensure free education for blind people.

The Relief Commission paid a blind man $50 a month, while a blind woman received $30. An adult who lost the sight of one eye received $30 a year.

Totally or partially blind children did not qualify for a pension. Instead, the commission paid their board at the School for the Blind or paid teachers for special classes.

CHAPTER 6

RECOVERY, RELIEF AND RECONSTRUCTION

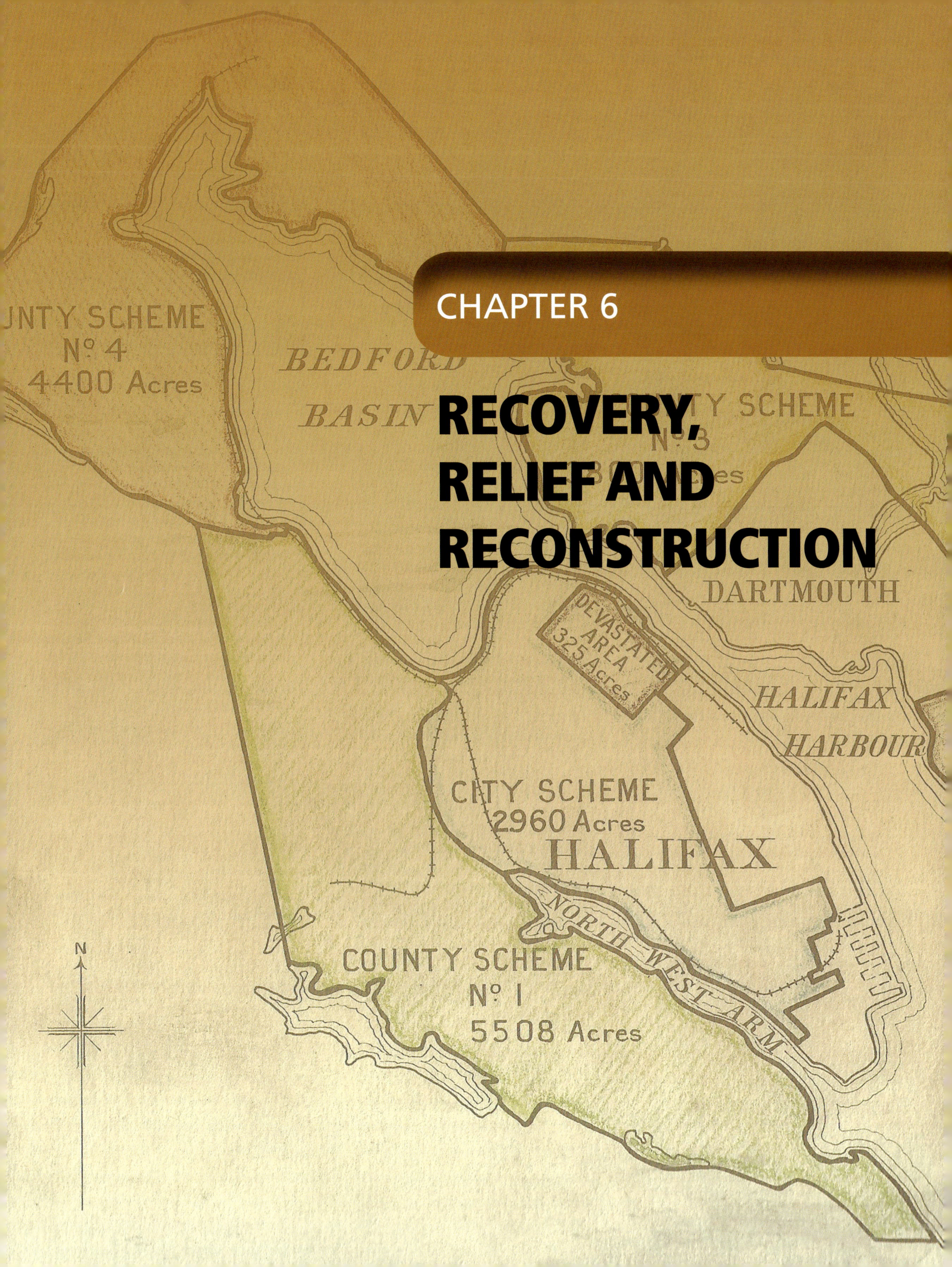

RECOVERY OF THE DEAD

The band of the Princess Louise Fusiliers prepares to play at a public funeral service for the unidentified dead of all denominations, December 17. White children's coffins are nearest the camera.

Five private undertakers worked in the two communities: three in Halifax and two in Dartmouth.

Because these firms could not even begin to cope with the dead, the mortuary committee established a temporary morgue in a central location for unidentified and unclaimed bodies. This arrangement would also make it easier for people searching for lost loved ones.

Officials selected the basement of the Chebucto Road School (today the Maritime Conservatory of Performing Arts) as the morgue's location. As soon as word got out and even before it was ready for use, bodies started to arrive, stacked outside the building until army engineers completed repairs.

Once its doors opened on December 7, soldiers began to deliver corpses from hospitals, undertakers and the devastated area. Embalmers came from across the province and further away to assist overwhelmed local ones.

The grim lessons of the 1912 *Titanic* tragedy came back and, using procedures developed then, the mortuary committee established methods to identify the dead. Arthur Barnstead, in charge of the mortuary committee, was the son of the man who undertook the same job when *Titanic* victims came to Halifax.

Each body was numbered, described and an exact record made of where it was found.

Most of the bodies recovered from Richmond were burnt to some degree.

Sometimes, the only entry made was "charred remains," or similar wording. Workers carefully catalogued personal effects and put them into numbered mortuary bags, along with any undamaged clothing.

A contractor's report details finding "charred human remains" at 95 Albert Street during the clearance of the north end, which were "sent to Mortuary."

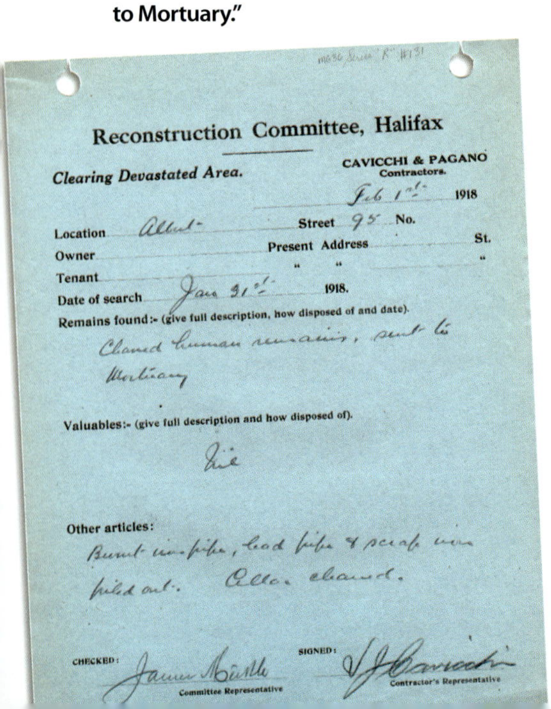

Reconstruction Committee, Halifax

Clearing Devastated Area. CAVICCHI & PAGANO Contractors.

Feb 1st 1918

Location Albert Street 95 No.

Owner Present Address St.

Tenant

Date of search Jan 31st 1918.

Remains found:- (give full description, how disposed of and date).

Charred human remains, sent to Mortuary

Valuables:- (give full description and how disposed of).

Nil

Other articles:

Burnt iron pipe, lead pipe & scrap iron piled out. Cellar cleaned.

CHECKED: Committee Representative SIGNED: Contractor's Representative

Morgue Memories

An anonymous Irish-American volunteer for Britain's Irish Guards, waiting transport overseas, was pressed into morgue duty along with his comrades. He recorded his memories of the event: "A gruesome, nauseating job; trying to identify those poor victims by arranging any little scrap of evidence that could be found on them…In a great many cases it was utterly impossible to identify any of them for the condition they were in. The heart-rending scenes witnessed there will live in my memory as long as I live…To witness these relatives and friends as they walked past the long lines of victims stretched out in rows…was a sad sight. There would be a scream here, a moan or a sob there; then someone would have to be carried away from that terrible scene…but we kept on at our unpleasant task of trying to arrange the poor creatures in such a way that they could be placed in wooden boxes to await burial later…"

The weather was very bad; rain, snow, sleet and strong winds all of the time; with intense cold. We dug long lines of trenches in this inclement weather, to bury the dead in, and when we returned to our huts at night we would have to hang our wet clothes around two old stoves in the hut to dry them out, if only a little, so we could wear them the next day."

As many as 70 soldiers assisted this daily work at the morgue. Another 25 to 50 servicemen formed digging and covering-in parties at various cemeteries on a daily basis.

Soon, a steady stream of ambulances, wagons and private cars arrived at its doors, laden with the dead, from 9 a.m. to 10 p.m. daily.

Another continuous lineup also formed quickly: thousands of apprehensive relatives searching for their loved ones. Once bodies were positively identified, they were released to families for burial, unless they could not afford it, in which case the mortuary committee took responsibility.

Roman Catholic priests conduct a funeral mass for unidentified dead outside the Chebucto Road morgue, December 17.

BURIALS

Burials of unidentified bodies began on December 17.

Ninety-five badly charred remains were interred that day.

The funeral service took place beforehand in the Chebucto Road schoolyard, witnessed by about 3,000 people. To the music of the Princess Louise Fusiliers band, soldiers carried wreath-adorned caskets from the basement and laid them in rows outside.

Protestant and Roman Catholic services followed. Afterward, soldiers loaded the coffins onto trucks, took them to the Fairview or Mount Olivet Cemeteries and placed them in waiting graves.

Additional burials took place until Christmas Eve.

Authorities buried a large number of unidentified remains in a bare patch of ground next to the new railway cutting through the western side of the peninsula toward the new station.

Today, four lanes of traffic on Bayer's Road whiz by the site, unknown and unseen by drivers and their passengers.

The Last Body

Given its eight stories collapsed in a mass of rubble, it could be expected the last known body to be recovered was found in the wreckage of the Acadia Sugar Refinery, at the time the tallest building in Canada east of Montreal. The body of Vincent Pattison, 54, who worked as an engineer at the refinery, was not found until April 1918. Officials returned his personal effects to his wife, Catherine, and buried his remains in Mount Olivet Cemetery. Among the items returned was their son James's pocket watch, which Vincent had borrowed because his was being repaired. The watch was stopped at 9:10 a.m. As the family knew, it always ran a few minutes fast.

More bodies continued to be found until well into the spring, when workers completed proper clearance of the wreckage.

In the end, about 250 bodies remained unidentified.

TO THE MEMORY OF THE UNIDENTIFIED DEAD VICTIMS OF THE GREAT DISASTER DECEMBER 6, 1917

Inscription, Bayer's Road Memorial.

City residents line up outside the Halifax Armouries on North Park Street to collect food.

TEMPORARY ARRANGEMENTS

Once officials met the survivors' immediate needs for medical aid, food, clothing and shelter, there remained the greater problem of the creation of some form of lasting accommodation for those who had lost their homes.

Repairs were quickly completed on lightly damaged homes outside the north end. By January 21, repairs to 3,000 damaged homes had been carried out, some by their owners and others by workmen as building materials became available. Such repairs usually consisted of new windows and doors, plus a chimney inspection to make sure it was safe to use.

The new Imperial Oil refinery was under construction a few kilometres from the blast site across the harbour. No damage was done to the refinery, but the force of the explosion threw several workmen to the ground. The refinery's management responded immediately and rushed workers and all movable construction material to Halifax and Dartmouth to provide shelter for the injured and homeless—at no charge.

In the work camps at the new community of Imperoyal next door, the men doubled up to provide accommodation and care for 160 homeless people, including some 50 to 60 children. The employees took up a collection and provided the homeless with a Christmas present. Early in 1918 relief operations had progressed to the point where accommodation was found elsewhere and construction personnel went back to building the refinery.

Many homes in the central devastated area of Halifax completely disappeared or were beyond repair; something more permanent was required. At the time, authorities estimated almost 8,000 people still needed accommodation.

Although the Relief Committee did yeoman work, it soon became evident a more permanent body would have to be established to oversee the massive reconstruction that faced the city. Consequently, on January 22 by an Order-in-Council under the War Measures Act, the Dominion government appointed the Halifax Relief Commission to replace the temporary Halifax Relief Committee.

HALIFAX RELIEF COMMISSION

Dominion and later provincial legislation gave the commission wide powers to rebuild the devastated areas. This occasionally placed the commission at odds with both the local municipal governments and private citizens.

Halifax Relief Commission Members

Chairman: Tecumseh Sherman Rogers, King's Counsel (K.C.), prominent Halifax lawyer.

Member: William Bernard Wallace, Halifax County Court Judge.

Member: Frederick Luther Fowke, Oshawa, Ontario businessman.

Secretary: Ralph Pickard Bell, Halifax businessman.

Its mandate included the management of all aspects of the relief effort, which included funding, the work of volunteer committees already established, reporting on damage and finding "the best method of restoring or assisting in the restoration of the area affected." It had nearly $21 million in donations to carry out its job, over which it seems to have had absolute control.

The Dominion government also selected Colonel Robert Low, who designed and built military camps during the war, to oversee the work of reconstruction. Low built 832 temporary tenement-style apartments at four sites. Three were in Halifax—at the Exhibition Grounds on Almon St., the Garrison Grounds on Sackville St. and the South Common on Bell Road—and one was in Dartmouth, near Victoria Park.

The commission brought in building equipment, supplies, horses and 2,200 workers and housed them at the Exhibition Grounds. Local construction companies hired to assist brought in an additional 1,500 workers.

These temporary buildings—designed to last for five years—were constructed of wood and tarpaper, finished inside with beaverboard and equipped with water, sewage and electricity. Builders completed apartments at the rate of one per hour, with the first ones ready for occupancy on the South Common in 30 days. They housed 1,000 people.

Minor strikes delayed progress. Unions complained some tradesmen were employed outside their occupation—such as plasterers laying bricks—and no overtime was paid for Sunday work. The commission promised better conditions once the worst of the housing crisis passed.

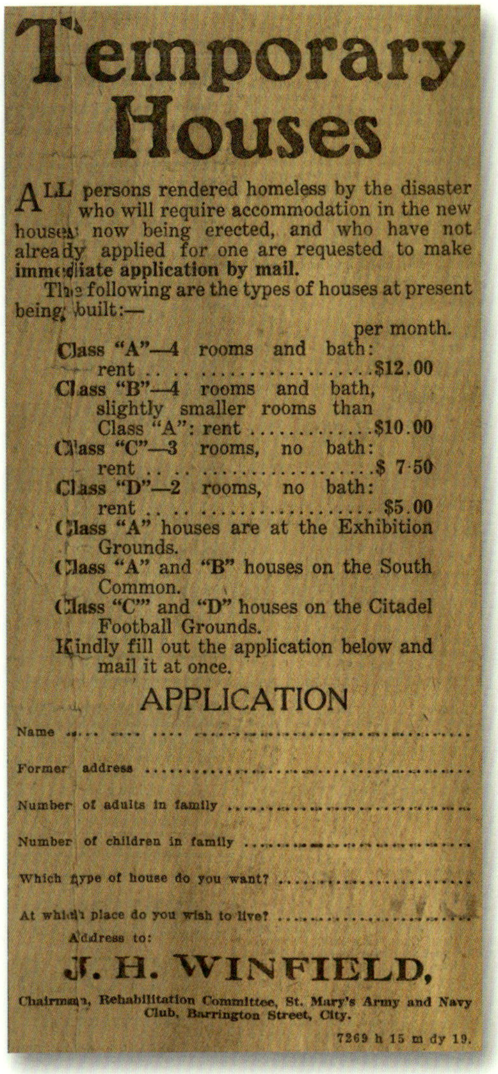

Temporary Houses

ALL persons rendered homeless by the disaster who will require accommodation in the new houses now being erected, and who have not already applied for one are requested to make immediate application by mail.

The following are the types of houses at present being built:—

per month.

Class "A"—4 rooms and bath: rent $12.00

Class "B"—4 rooms and bath, slightly smaller rooms than Class "A": rent $10.00

Class "C"—3 rooms, no bath: rent ....$ 7.50

Class "D"—2 rooms, no bath: rent $5.00

Class "A" houses are at the Exhibition Grounds.

Class "A" and "B" houses on the South Common.

Class "C" and "D" houses on the Citadel Football Grounds.

Kindly fill out the application below and mail it at once.

APPLICATION

Name ....

Former address ....

Number of adults in family ....

Number of children in family ....

Which type of house do you want? ....

At which place do you wish to live? ....

Address to:

J. H. WINFIELD,

Chairman, Rehabilitation Committee, St. Mary's Army and Navy Club, Barrington Street, City.

7269 h 15 m dy 19.

Elsewhere, workmen built 40 two-storey apartment buildings containing 320 apartments, four apartment blocks containing 16 flats each and temporary stables.

(top): A mail-in application for temporary housing advertises accommodation of various sizes, with and without bath, at three sites in Halifax.

(bottom): The Governor McCall Apartments opened on the Exhibition Grounds in March 1918 and housed 2,200 people.

In mid-March, another group of buildings opened on the Exhibition Grounds, where about 2,200 people moved in. To honour the relief provided by Massachusetts, officials named these buildings the Governor McCall Apartments after the governor of the state.

The Massachusetts-Halifax Relief Fund provided furnishings for free, which included not only furniture, but also items such as linens and cutlery. Families who moved into this accommodation chose their furniture from a variety of styles and could keep it even when they vacated the temporary buildings. Rents ranged from $5 per month for a two-room flat to $12 per month for four rooms. For many displaced families, their temporary accommodation was an improvement over their previous living conditions.

Some of those not in receipt of items from the Massachusetts fund complained. As a result, the commission began to deduct the cost of any furnishings provided from monetary claims.

(top): The Massachusetts-Halifax Relief Committee distributed furniture free of charge to residents of temporary housing from this warehouse.

(below): A lease signed on May 1, 1919, for a new house rented to Thaddeus and Mary McTiernan for $28 a month. The house still exists today at the corner of Robie and Young Streets.

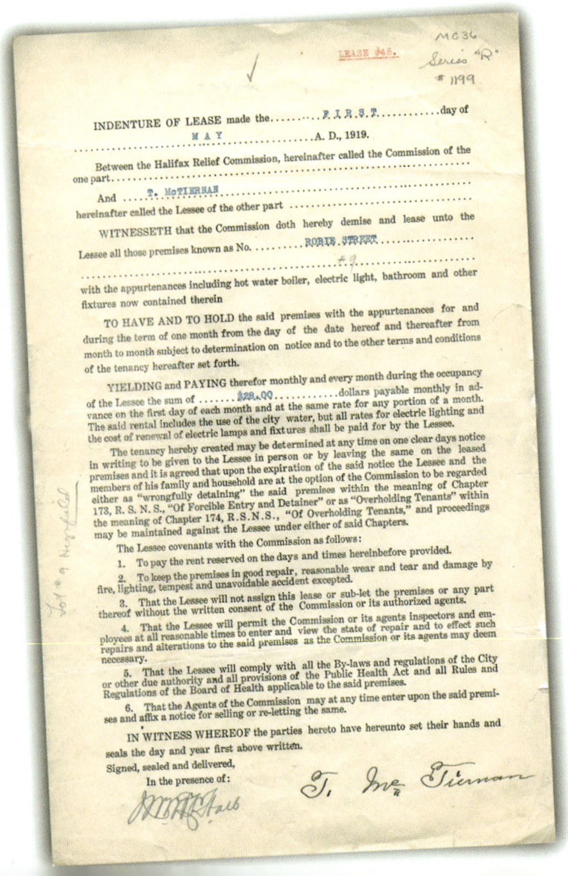

MC36
Series "R"
1199

LEASE #45.

INDENTURE OF LEASE made the..........FIRST..........day of MAY..........A. D., 1919.

Between the Halifax Relief Commission, hereinafter called the Commission of the one part..........

And ....T. McTIERNAN..........
hereinafter called the Lessee of the other part ....

WITNESSETH that the Commission doth hereby demise and lease unto the Lessee all those premises known as No. ....ROBIE STREET..........
..........#9..........
with the appurtenances including hot water boiler, electric light, bathroom and other fixtures now contained therein

TO HAVE AND TO HOLD the said premises with the appurtenances for and during the term of one month from the day of the date hereof and thereafter from month to month subject to determination on notice and to the other terms and conditions of the tenancy hereafter set forth.

YIELDING and PAYING therefor monthly and every month during the occupancy of the Lessee the sum of ....$28.00..........dollars payable monthly in advance on the first day of each month and at the same rate for any portion of a month. The said rental includes the use of the city water, but all rates for electric lighting and the cost of renewal of electric lamps and fixtures shall be paid for by the Lessee.

The tenancy hereby created may be determined at any time on one clear days notice in writing to be given to the Lessee in person or by leaving the same on the leased premises and it is agreed that upon the expiration of the said notice the Lessee and the members of his family and household are at the option of the Commission to be regarded either as "wrongfully detaining" the said premises within the meaning of Chapter 173, R. S. N. S., "Of Forcible Entry and Detainer" or as "Overholding Tenants" within the meaning of Chapter 174, R.S.N.S., "Of Overholding Tenants," and proceedings may be maintained against the Lessee under either of said Chapters.

The Lessee covenants with the Commission as follows:

1. To pay the rent reserved on the days and times hereinbefore provided.
2. To keep the premises in good repair, reasonable wear and tear and damage by fire, lighting, tempest and unavoidable accident excepted.
3. That the Lessee will not assign this lease or sub-let the premises or any part thereof without the written consent of the Commission or its authorized agents.
4. That the Lessee will permit the Commission or its agents inspectors and employees at all reasonable times to enter and view the state of repair and to effect such repairs and alterations to the said premises as the Commission or its agents may deem necessary.
5. That the Lessee will comply with all the By-laws and regulations of the City or other due authority and all provisions of the Public Health Act and all Rules and Regulations of the Board of Health applicable to the said premises.
6. That the Agents of the Commission may at any time enter upon the said premises and affix a notice for selling or re-letting the same.

IN WITNESS WHEREOF the parties hereto have hereunto set their hands and seals the day and year first above written.

Signed, sealed and delivered,
In the presence of:

T. McTiernan

RELIEF

The commission paid out claims for compensation for losses of personal belongings, ranging from destroyed or damaged clothing and furniture to lost merchandise. Claims were heard in two courts and overseen by lawyers. They rendered decisions quickly, with payment from what the recipients simply called "The Relief."

The courts normally paid claims for less than $100 the same day, while larger claims might entail additional visits to court.

Authorities rarely paid the full amounts requested, usually deducting a percentage.

Loss of cash and items considered a "pure luxury"—jewellery, fur coats, art work, ornaments, pianos—were not reimbursed. The loss of a car could be claimed; some objected to this, as they considered an automobile a pure luxury.

Human jealousy reared its ugly head again. When some residents became aware of how much their neighbours received—whether exaggerated or not—they felt short-changed.
In the end, the commission paid $2,570,048.60 against 16,422 claims totalling $3,494,730.11; 74 per cent of the total. Small businesses fared slightly better. The $258,327.05 paid for 1,156 claims represented 77 per cent of the total requested.

The commission also paid out property claims for private homes and small businesses, starting with claims under $5,000. In the case of total destruction, owners could rebuild at the expense of the commission or receive a lump sum equal to the appraised value.

For damaged houses, owners could choose between having commission builders do the work, hire someone privately for reimbursement or sell it to the commission. During the first year, several thousand houses were repaired.

Payment of property claims also received complaints, usually due to undervaluation vis-a-vis escalating replacement costs.

It took until early summer 1919 before the commission heard claims for property worth more than $5,000—all of them for businesses.

PENSIONS

Another aspect of the commission's work was the establishment of a pension plan for those who could no longer earn a living due to their injuries or who suffered permanent disabilities. After considerable study, the commission based their plan on the military's (although servicemen were ineligible), and prorated payments based on previous family income, but also considered individual family circumstances.

The commission paid the first pensions in May. Amputees, the blind and the partially sighted received special assistance, as did widows with children to enable them to find jobs. One hundred orphans received pensions until age 17 or earlier if they left school. Women whose morality was questioned could lose their pension for six months. A second cancellation resulted in a permanent loss.

The commission also offered lump-sum payments in lieu of pensions, based on age and extent of disabilities. Any pensions, grants or allowances received with respect to an explosion-related death or injury were never subject to income tax.

In the first four years, the commission paid out $1 million in pensions and lump-sum payments.

Both payouts and pensions had their critics. The social mores of the day clearly influenced decisions. Families deemed "respectable" received more than poor people. Soldiers' wives—either married or common law—and Africville residents were treated unfairly. In the latter case, blacks received a lower percentage of the amount of their claims than most whites.

Even the distribution of clothing and food received complaints.

Victims did not want second-hand clothing and there was not enough black clothing available for those in mourning. Those not in receipt of a food allowance complained those who received it did not spend all of it on food.

As a result, officials issued no more second-hand clothing—except where they deemed new clothing "inappropriate" for the victims' former financial status—and they decreased the food allowance by one-quarter to one-half.

Some people also claimed others received preferential treatment to obtain accommodation.

When the Commission finally disbanded in June 1976, 66 pensioners were still receiving monthly payments. Responsibility for payment was then transferred to the Department of Veterans' Affairs (now Veterans' Affairs Canada).

The last year the department distributed pensions was 2010, after the last client died in June of that year.

At the time, no money remained in the pension fund.

Halifax Relief Commission houses under construction at the corner of Kaye and Robie Streets, which still stand today.

REDEVELOPMENT

Despite the temporary arrangements to house the homeless, something more permanent was required to replace some of the 750 houses either completely destroyed or damaged beyond repair. The Relief Commission hired a famed Scottish pioneer in urban planning, Thomas Adams—then employed in Ottawa—and his assistant, Horace L. Seymour, to develop a new master plan

The living room of one of the Governor McCall Apartments, containing furniture supplied by the Massachusetts-Halifax Relief Committee.

for Richmond and design some houses. Adams specialized in designing low-density residential developments, commonly referred to as "garden cities."

The garden city movement, initiated in Britain in 1898, saw garden cities as planned, self-contained communities, surrounded by greenbelts and containing proportionate areas of residences, industry and agriculture. The commission contracted George Ross, a partner in one of Canada's most notable architectural firms at the time, Ross and Macdonald of Montreal, to carry out Adams's scheme.

Thomas Adams, the Scottish-born town planner who conceived the idea for the redevelopment of the north end. His original proposal encompassed all of Halifax and Dartmouth, as well as large parts of Halifax County.

Initially, Adams's vision of redevelopment extended to the entire north end and beyond. It encompassed not only all of Halifax and Dartmouth, but also large portions of Halifax County that surrounded the core area like a giant horseshoe. In the end, the commission adopted his plan for only the 132 hectares (325 acres) under its jurisdiction, designated the area of total devastation and the area severe damage. Together, these areas stretched from Robie Street on the west, eastwards to the harbour, and from Russell Street on the south, northwards to about where Merv Sullivan Park is today.

Adams's proposal superimposed two 25-metre (80-feet)- wide diagonal avenues—Devonshire and Dartmouth Avenues—on the already existing street plan. These would link Gottingen and Barrington Streets, with squares where they met for public buildings, In the end, only Devonshire was completed for its full length and Dartmouth became a mere shadow of Adams's original proposal. Additionally, Adams added rounded streets to ring Needham Hill, where land was also obtained to create a new public park.

HYDROSTONE

Adams's solution also included the imaginative—and controversial at the time—Hydrostone project. Many regarded this development on 9.3 hectares (23 acres) expropriated at Merkel's field, a flat, low-lying area immediately west of Fort Needham, as unjust, extravagant and impractical. The Hydrostone District was both central to and the centre of the area controlled by the commission.

An Eastern Passage brickyard produced the concrete blocks used to rebuild much of Halifax's shattered north end. The project was named after the concrete blocks used to build the new houses—Hydrostone—the trade name of a Chicago company that developed the process. Hydrostone blocks were made of gravel or crushed stone, sand, Portland cement and water molded under 68,040 kilograms (150,000 pounds) of pressure, which forced excess moisture to the surface.

Financial Donations

In addition to immediate donations of medical supplies, food, clothing, building materials and other desperately needed items, financial support poured into Halifax from all levels of government from around the world. As well, several companies and the general public donated funds for Halifax's relief. These funds quickly reached about $21 million--later rising to $30 million—against property losses estimated at $35 million. All monies were put into the hands of the Relief Commission. Among the donations:

Canada: $18,000,000

Britain: $4,815,000 (£1,000,000)

United States: $5,000,000

Massachusetts (goods & money): $750,000

London (individuals): $600,000

Australia: $250,000

British Red Cross: $125,000

Chicago: $125,000

Ontario: $100,000

Bank of Nova Scotia: $100,000

Manitoba (governments & individuals): $100,000

New Zealand: $50,000

Imperial Oil: $10,000

Compagnie Générale Transatlantique: $10,000

King George V: $5,000

Newfoundland: $5,000

(top): A crane loads Hydrostone blocks onto a scow in January 1919, to transport them from their Eastern Passage plant across the harbour, where they will be put on a temporary railway spur to be delivered to the construction site.

(left): Workman build a Hydrostone house, March 1919.

HYDRO-STONE

The Material Used in Rebuilding Halifax

as specified by Ross & Macdonald, Architects.

HYDRO-STONE was used in the erection of over 300 houses of permanent construction, and no other material would have answered the requirements so well as HYDRO-STONE.

The views reproduced show a block of HYDRO-STONE just delivered from the machine and blocks being loaded on cars for shipment from the yards at Halifax to the building lots.

HYDRO-STONE is a building unit made of properly proportioned aggregate, consisting of gravel or crushed stone, sand and Portland cement, with sufficient water to crystallize it thoroughly. In the making, each unit is subjected to 150,000 pounds pressure, resulting in a unit that has a smaller percentage of absorption than any other building material. This pressure forces the excess moisture to the surface at all points and compacts the aggregates so closely that a perfect bond is insured, giving maximum density and strength.

HYDRO-STONE is hardened in wet live steam, which causes all the moisture to be retained until thorough crystallization has taken place. This results in a hard dense concrete unit with sharp, clean edges.

Made in any size, shape or design desired. Any color scheme can be followed with excellent results. You should investigate this new and important building material. Send for particulars.

HYDRO-STONE COMPANY

Second Floor Insurance Building

Chicago, Illinois

A Block for Every Wall
A Wall for Every Purpose

This resulted in compacted blocks of great density and strength. The blocks were hardened with steam and then faced with sand or crushed granite, which made them sparkle.

The blocks each weighed 36 kilograms (80 pounds). They were light enough to be lifted and laid without the need for cranes or wall forms, and stucco bonded easily to their surface. But their most important quality was fire resistance, which made them highly desirable after the explosion, both physically and psychologically. Wooden houses that collapsed usually knocked over coal or wood stoves, adding vast amounts of fuel to the fires.

The factory established in Eastern Passage manufactured as many as 4,000 Hydrostone blocks a day, with sand and gravel from Barrie Beach in South East Passage. It was located about halfway between the Crick (today's Fisherman's Cove) and Hartlen Point, on a site where the Nova Scotia Construction Company produced concrete for several years, with the same Barrie Beach sand and gravel to make concrete for the piles at the Halifax docks.

Construction started in September 1918. When completed, the rectangular Hydrostone District was more than 800 metres (half a mile) long, but only 128 metres (420 feet) wide. It comprised 328 individual dwellings spread across 10 parallel blocks and housed about 2,000 people. The units ranged from houses and apartments of four-and-a-half rooms to six or seven rooms.

The first 24 houses were ready in March 1919. The plan was that another 20 would be finished every two weeks. However, it took until mid-1921 before all units were completed, largely due to labour disputes. Manpower shortages in the summer of 1919 led the commission to use non-union labour, which displeased the unions.

The commission averted a probable strike when it threatened to publicize the reason for it. Faced with a potential public backlash, the unions backed down.

There were single dwellings, as well as others joined in blocks of two, four or six units. All of them vaguely resembled English mock Tudor-style homes. A small commercial strip on Young Street consisted of 15 stores and three offices. Rents varied from $25 per month for a four-room apartment to $50 for a seven-room house. On January 1, 1949, the Relief Commission began selling them for $2,500 to $3,500 each, depending on their size, a process completed in 1955. In 1993, the federal government designated the Hydrostone District a National Historic Site of Canada.

Many homes were also rebuilt outside the Hydrostone District and several of these used house plans designed by Ross's architectural firm.

(opposite): An advertisement from *Construction: A Journal for the Architectural, Engineering and Contracting Interests of Canada*, October 1919.

(below) The ceremonial opening of a block of Hydrostone houses, April 19, 1920.

Fact Sheet: Richmond's Churches and Schools

For the tightly knit, largely working class community of Richmond, its churches and schools played an important part in the area's social life.

Churches

Richmond contained four churches, all built within a six-year period—and all destroyed by the explosion.

-St. Joseph's Roman Catholic (1867) on Gottingen Street included a school and a convent, with Father Charles McManus as priest. The explosion left only two walls of St. Joseph's standing, damaged it beyond repair and killed 404 of its parishioners.

The ruins of St. Joseph's Roman Catholic Church.

A basement church was built on the site in 1920, with the rest of the church completed in 1961. The new St. Joseph's was demolished in 2008, two years after the parish joined with St. Stephen's and became St. Mother Teresa of Kolkata Parish, using the former St. Stephen's Church.

-St. Mark's Anglican (1866) on Russell Street was overseen by the Reverend N. Lemoine. It had been enlarged twice to accommodate additional naval and military personnel who moved into the area as a result of the war. The explosion collapsed the church, which then burned. About 200 members of its congregation were killed. St. Mark's was rebuilt in 1921.

The new United Memorial Church on Kaye Street, shortly after its completion in 1921.

-Grove Presbyterian (1872), on the northern slope of Fort Needham on Duffus Street, was under the care of the Reverend Charles Crowdis, who lived in the manse nearby on Gottingen Street. The church lost 170 of its parishioners.

-Kaye Street Methodist (1869) sat on the southern slope of Fort Needham. Reverend William Swetnam lived in its parsonage across the road on Young Street. The explosion killed 167 of its members.

While new churches were built, Richmond's parishioners accepted the hospitality of other churches and worshipped with their congregations. The first service held in Richmond after the explosion was held jointly by Methodists and Presbyterians in a temporary tarpaper building at the corner of Young and Gottingen streets on March 17, 1918. The Methodists and Presbyterians initially formed the Kaye-Grove Church, where each denomination held its own services under its own pastor. Eventually, the two merged and in 1920 changed their name to the United Memorial Church—a predecessor of the United Church of Canada formed four years later by a merger of Methodists, Presbyterians and Congregationalists. The new church was completed in 1921. Catholics and Anglicans even worshipped together for a short time, an early but short-lived example of ecumenism in a city normally divided along religious lines.

Schools

Children in Richmond attended three schools, two of which were destroyed and one damaged.

-St. Joseph's Roman Catholic School on Gottingen Street was normally only for girls, but as the boy's school had burned down in 1916, Catholic boys went there temporarily while their new school—the Alexander McKay—was built on Russell Street. To keep the sexes apart, the girls went to classes in the morning, with afternoons reserved for boys. The explosion caved in the ceilings and blew out the windows, which required the school to be rebuilt. Eight girls were killed—four of them later from their injuries—while another 15 absentees also died. Among the boys, 55 lost their lives. The partially built Alexander McKay needed substantial repairs.

The Alexander McKay School, which was still under construction, suffered damage in the explosion.

-Richmond School on Roome Street commenced winter hours a few days earlier, with classes starting at 9:30 a.m., a half hour later than usual. Because of this change, only two pupils were killed in the school, which was destroyed, although 86 other students died, many on their way to school.

-Bloomfield School on Agricola was severely damaged and required extensive repairs.

CHAPTER 7

GUILTY UNTIL PROVEN INNOCENT—AND THEN STILL GUILTY

SABOTEURS?

Within hours of the explosion, Haligonians and others anxiously waited to discover what caused the death and destruction that had descended on their city—and to assign blame. The first thought for many people was a German naval fleet had bombarded the city from offshore or a Zeppelin had dropped bombs from the air.

Some survivors even swore they saw German soldiers in the streets.

Since the outbreak of the war in 1914, many blamed Germans for the global conflict. They were disliked and viewed with suspicion; those living in Canada had to report to the authorities once a month. Conspiracy theorists were alive and well even 100 years ago, claiming German spies and saboteurs were behind the explosion. Many residents believed the same: German fifth columnists were at work and orchestrated this "attack."

"My very first memory was 1917, the Halifax Explosion. I was three years old and I was having my breakfast, sitting in a high chair thing in the kitchen when it happened and of course we thought that we were being attacked...But do you know what my first memory was? Absolutely fascinating. It shows at three how much a little child will absorb, what they hear their older people saying around them. I saw—I didn't of course—but I thought I saw the Germans marching up the foot of Inglis Street—there's a little hill—and they were in their gray uniforms with helmets and that is my first memory. 'Course it was my imagination at that point."

Janet Piers, transcribed from a video interview in December 2009, when she was 95 years old.

German soldiers casually stroll down the street of an occupied town.

A few even thought a second one would follow within days.

Germans living in Halifax were stoned and chased through the streets by angry mobs, while some even had their homes attacked and windows smashed. Others were jailed, although later released without charge.

The times were far more xenophobic than today. Anyone who spoke a foreign language—or had difficulty with English—was deemed untrustworthy. This even extended to surviving crewmen of *Mont-Blanc* and *Imo*, who spoke a hodgepodge of languages.

It did not help that most of *Mont-Blanc*'s sailors were French, whom many residents associated with Quebec and the strong anti-conscription sentiments in that province. Additionally—in the opinion of many English Canadians—French Canadians did not contribute fully to the war effort.

Yellow journalism was alive and well at the time, and journalists, editors and publishers did not hesitate to stir up their readers with falsehoods, exaggerated rumours and scare-mongering.

Adding "foreigners" to the mix created a volatile brew. The newspapers reported on the explosion inquiry as if it were a trial and further inflamed public opinion by suggesting another explosion could occur at any time as effective control of harbour traffic had still not been established.

The *Imo*'s injured helmsman, John Johansen, was even kept under armed guard in the hospital for a time, as he was erroneously thought to be a German spy. The other surviving and uninjured crewmen from *Mont-Blanc* and *Imo* required for the inquiry were accommodated in *Highflyer*.

(opposite): A British poster outlines the differences between German and British airships and airplanes for the information of the general public.

"So long as there are people in Halifax who remember this past week or whose children remember it so long will the name German be a name for loathing and distrust."

Halifax Herald editorial, December 12, 1917.

A stoic young child shows facial injuries typical of explosion victims.

British civilians inside the wreckage of their house after a German Zeppelin dropped a bomb nearby.

INQUIRY CONVENED

In this charged atmosphere, the Dominion Minister of Marine and Fisheries, Charles Ballantyne, convened a Wreck Commissioner's Inquiry under the Canada Shipping Act, which was to be "instituted without delay" on Prime Minister Sir Robert Borden's direction. The inquiry was a routine procedure required wherever damage or loss to ships or other marine facilities occurred. Because criminal or civil charges could result from such an inquiry, it was conducted like a trial, with lawyers representing the various parties and allowed to cross-examine witnesses.

A chairman headed the inquiry, assisted by two nautical assessors to advise the judge and use their technical and marine knowledge to examine witnesses in areas in which lawyers might be unfamiliar.

Wreck Commission Members

Chairman: Arthur Drysdale, local judge in Admiralty for the Nova Scotia District of the Exchequer Court of Canada and a judge of the Supreme Court of Nova Scotia. Born in New Annan in 1857, Drysdale was admitted to the bar in 1882 and appointed K.C. in 1893. He was president of the Barristers' Society in 1904 and represented Hants County as a Liberal Member of the Legislative Assembly from 1891 to 1907, serving as commissioner of public works and mines (1901-05) and attorney general (1905-07). Drysdale was named to the Supreme Court of Nova Scotia in 1907, appointed deputy judge of the Admiralty Court in 1909 and local judge in Admiralty in 1912.

"He was a prominent figure at the bar, a very able politician, and one of the cleverest public speakers in Nova Scotia."

David Allison and Clyde Edwin Tuck, *History of Nova Scotia, Volume 3*, 1916.

Nautical Assessor: Acting Captain Walter Hose, RCN, captain of patrols for the east coast from August 1917 and briefly in command of the Dockyard after the explosion. A naval career was probably pre-ordained for Hose, having been born at sea aboard the P&O steamer *Surat* in the Indian Ocean in 1875. He joined the RN at 14, advanced through the ranks and held six commands before becoming executive officer in HMS *Cochrane*, a Warrior class armoured cruiser, in 1909. He thought promotion too slow in the RN and transferred to the RCN in 1912, two years after it was established and after a period on loan to the fledgling service. He commanded HMCS *Rainbow* on the west coast before moving to the east coast.

"In adversity, neither politics, lack of money, nor ridicule could beat the determination and courage of this officer."

Inscription on Walter Hose Monument, Point Pleasant Park, Halifax.

Nautical Assessor: Captain Leander (Louis) Demers, Wreck Commissioner for Canada. Demers was born in Montreal in 1862 and went to sea at 16, apprenticed to a shipping firm. He served on sailing ships and became chief officer of the famous clipper ship *Thermopylae* in 1886, sailing from Australia and China to London, where he set many records. He then joined the Canadian Marine Department, where he held various appointments, including deputy wreck commissioner. He founded the Marine School in Montreal, the first in Canada, which was followed by several others. He was appointed wreck commissioner in 1912.

"A man of outstanding knowledge and sound judgement."

Obituary, *Ottawa Citizen*, July 11, 1938.

Left:
(top): Acting Captain Walter Hose.
(centre): Judge Arthur Drysdale.
(bottom): Captain Louis Demers.

INQUIRY OPENED

The Halifax County Court House where the explosion inquiry was held from December 13, 1917-January 29, 1918, with a month-long break from December 21-January 21.

(below): Although *Imo's* lawyer, Charles Burchell, continuously violated most of the rules of proper courtroom etiquette, inquiry chairman Judge Arthur Drysdale did not intervene.

The inquiry opened on December 13 in Courtroom No. 1 at the County Court House on Spring Garden Road, in a high-ceilinged room that still showed the effects of the explosion. Boards covered the windows and dim light came from two oil lamps. The inquiry called Captain Le Médec as the first witness, which was immediately objected to by *Mont-Blanc*'s lawyers.

Drysdale overruled the objection. Proceedings went downhill from there.

The ships' owners blamed each other.

Harbour officials blamed the navy.

The navy blamed the pilots.

The general conduct of the inquiry was marked by procedures and comments not permitted today: loose cross-examinations, false accusations, badgering and misleading witnesses, misquoting participants, speculative scenarios, biased comments and hearsay evidence presented as fact.

Charles Burchell claimed to be at a disadvantage as both the captain and pilot of *Imo*, which he represented, were dead. With pilots a key factor in the accident, he thought Hayes should have a lawyer. Drysdale directed him to fill that capacity for the morning and find someone else at noon if he thought it necessary.

The wily Burchell quickly realized the advantage this position offered him and never did find another lawyer, continuing to represent Hayes throughout.

This was perhaps the first indication Drysdale had already made up his mind as to whom was at fault.

Wreck Commission Lawyers

A stable of lawyers represented the various factions involved:

- **Government of Canada:** William Henry, K.C., assembled the commission at the request of the Dominion government and acted as Crown counsel. He was responsible for organizing the proceedings and advising the court. Henry had also been one of the best all-round athletes in Canada.

- **Province of Nova Scotia:** Andrew Cluney, K.C., represented the attorney general of the province—who would be responsible for any criminal charges that might arise—and acted as Crown prosecutor.

- ***Mont-Blanc*:** Humphrey Mellish, K.C. had a distinguished legal career that began in 1890 and was about to be appointed judge. Joseph Nolan was a lawyer who worked for the Compagnie Générale Transatlantique in New York. He requested and was given the privileges of the Nova Scotia Bar for purposes of the inquiry.

- ***Imo*:** Charles Burchell, K.C., had an illustrious career in marine and commercial law, as well as being a talented all-round lawyer. He was known for unrelenting attacks against witnesses and was prepared to stretch the boundaries of proper courtroom conduct.

- **City of Halifax:** Frank Bell, K.C..

- **Halifax Pilotage Commission:** Thomas Robertson, K.C..

Le Médec was called to the stand, where much of his testimony centred on whistle blasts and their meanings. Whistles were also key to the accident, as the first ship that sounded a blast was normally in control of a navigational situation.

The sides representing the two vessels claimed different scenarios. Burchell maintained the first signal *Imo* heard was two blasts from *Mont-Blanc*, meaning she intended to cross, to which *Imo* responded with the same signal, meaning she agreed.

The combined force of the explosion and the tsunami beached *Imo* on the Dartmouth shore.

The French ship's witnesses stated *Mont-Blanc* gave one short blast first, telling *Imo* to move to her proper side, to which *Imo* replied with a double whistle—a cross-signal.

Other observers stated they heard *Imo*'s whistle first, but assumed it was meant for the tug, *Stella Maris*. The tug's crew disputed this interpretation.

Throughout, Le Médec steadfastly maintained he blew the first whistle, moved to starboard towards the Dartmouth shore and *Imo* blew a cross-signal in response.

Language caused a problem throughout the proceedings, as an interpreter for Le Médec altered between speaking of the French captain in the first and third person, while on some occasions he translated directly and on others he paraphrased testimony. The difference in navigational terms between French and English and whether or not Le Médec and Mackey understood each other clearly was also raised.

Compounding these differences was the unfamiliarity of the lawyers and some witnesses with nautical terminology. This latter point even extended at times to the nautical assessors and the judge, all of whom should have been thoroughly familiar with navigational terms due to their positions.

Burchell raised the issue of the red flag with Le Médec, suggesting he broke international law by not flying one, but the Frenchman successfully parried this line of questioning.

Burchell next turned to the evacuation of *Mont-Blanc*, claiming in the 20 minutes between collision and explosion the French crew had not warned anyone, but instead took to their lifeboats, their only priority being to save themselves. Although the crew could not possibly have known how much time they had before their ship would explode, the impression of the Frenchmen's cowardice or at least lack of gallantry—especially during wartime—quickly became implanted in the minds of many citizens.

Egged on by an already anti-French, vituperative press, this idea subtly turned the inquiry from its original aim of determining the cause of the collision to affixing blame for it.

Although Le Médec may have been justified in abandoning ship without any attempt at firefighting, many people believed there was no excuse for not taking a few seconds—at most a minute or two—to try to steer her, even without power—towards the uninhabited part of the Dartmouth shore and lock her helm before leaving, or warning other nearby ships and boats as he and his crew rowed away.

Yet, Le Médec steadfastly maintained it would not have minimized the danger to Halifax if he had tried to take the ship farther away from the city, such as to Bedford Basin.

Pilot Mackey agreed.

And, while the French captain answered all questions as straightforwardly as possible, it did not help that he appeared nervous throughout the inquiry.

Even worse, he never expressed regret or offered an apology for his actions.

INQUIRY CLOSED

Courtroom No. 1, where the explosion inquiry was held, photographed as Courtroom No. 4 today.

When the second day of the inquiry opened with Mackey in the stand, Drysdale stated he would allow lawyers some leeway during cross-examination, as long as they were clearly trying to find the truth.

This was all Burchell needed and he began to dominate the already acrimonious proceedings through ruthless cross-examination of several witnesses, prejudging *Mont-Blanc*'s crew as guilty. In this he was generally supported by public opinion and soon had Judge Drysdale on his side as well.

Objectivity flew out the window as Burchell hammered away day after day on the same theme: the French vessel was at fault.

Burchell even went so far as to contradict the testimony of his own witness, *Imo*'s second mate, Peter B'Jonnas. When the sailor said his ship's first blast was intended for the tug *Stella Maris* and not *Mont-Blanc*, the belligerent lawyer jumped to his feet and stated what B'Jonnas meant to say was the first signal he heard was two whistle blasts from *Mont-Blanc*.

He even invited Drysdale to question B'Jonnas himself about this information—a bizarre request if ever there were one. Burchell also insinuated Mackey was drunk as he piloted *Mont-Blanc*, a charge both the port warden and the Pilotage Commission chairman, who was also a sheriff, refuted.

Burchell's focus on *Mont-Blanc* diverted attention from the navy's responsibility for the disaster, much to the satisfaction of the Dominion government.

And so it went until January 29, 1918, with a lengthy break between December 21 and January 21. The sailors on both ships, crewmen from nearby vessels, spectators on land and other witnesses disagreed on most facts: where *Imo* and *Mont-Blanc* sailed through the harbour, how fast they were going, how many whistles and in what sequence they were blown by each ship, where and at what angle they collided and several other points.

During the 19 days it sat, the inquiry heard from 52 witnesses, whose testimony filled more than 2,100 pages. Judge Drysdale rendered his three-page, 13-point opinion on February 4. Interestingly, *Imo* was only mentioned once in Drysdale's judgement.

Drysdale's Findings

Judge Drysdale's less-than-impartial verdict came as a surprise to very few. He found:

- The explosion was the result of a collision between *Mont-Blanc* and *Imo*.
- The collision was caused by a violation of the rules of navigation.
- Captain Le Médec and Pilot Mackey were wholly responsible for violating the rules of the road.
- Le Médec and Mackey were guilty of neglect by failing to warn the public of a probable explosion.
- Acting Commander Wyatt was guilty of neglect for not taking proper steps to ensure harbour regulations were being followed and not keeping himself informed of ships' movements and intended movements.
- There was no satisfactory evidence Wyatt took proper action to inform the captain superintendent of the neglect by harbour pilots.
- The pilots' disobedience of Wyatt's orders was not the "proximate cause of the collision."

In addition, he recommended:

- Dismissal of Mackey by the pilotage authorities and revocation of his pilot's licence for gross negligence.
- Prosecution of Mackey in criminal court for this same negligence.
- Cancellation of Le Médec's master's papers by the French government and prosecution "according to the law of his country."
- Censure of pilotage authorities for failing to suspend Mackey's licence immediately after the collision.
- Censure of Pilot Renner, in charge of the American tramp steamer SS *Clara*, for varying well-known rules of the road.
- Competent naval authorities prepare specific regulations for handling ships "laden with explosives."

TRIALS AND TRIBULATIONS

The residents of Halifax greeted Drysdale's decisions with enthusiasm. Shortly afterwards, Wyatt, Le Médec and Mackey were arrested and charged with manslaughter in the death of *Imo*'s captain and her pilot, Haakon From and William Hayes. Le Médec made his $10,000 bail and Wyatt his $6,000 one, but Mackey could not come up with $6,000 for his and remained in the city jail.

After a preliminary hearing at which the judge found sufficient evidence to go to trial, the lawyer for Mackey filed a writ of habeas corpus (used to prevent unlawful detention), which resulted in the pilot's release. On March 15, 1918, Nova Scotia Supreme Court Judge Benjamin Russell heard the case.

He excluded testimony from the Wreck Commission, correctly reasoning it was an investigation and not a trial, and allowed seven new witnesses. Russell could not find any criminal behavior on the part of the trio and called their arrest a mistake.

Russell's unpopular decision was met with dismay and on March 19 a grand jury convened to evaluate Wyatt's criminal responsibility. A trial followed on April 16. Judge Russell again acquitted him of manslaughter and the additional charge of criminal negligence.

Concurrent with the inquiry, the owners of *Mont-Blanc* and *Imo* sued each other for $2 million. This case was heard in the Nova Scotia Division of the Exchequer Court of Canada and presided over by — Mr. Justice Arthur Drysdale! On April 27—as might be expected—he found *Mont-Blanc* solely to blame for the collision.

Mont-Blanc's owners then appealed his decision to the Supreme Court of Canada.

Before five judges of the Supreme Court, Charles Burchell again argued *Imo*'s case, while Hector McInnes represented *Mont-Blanc*. The hearing lasted for three days in March 1919, with a decision rendered two months later.

In their decision, the justices found the two ships equally at fault.

The pugilistic Burchell was unhappy with this ruling and appealed the decision to the Judicial Committee of the Privy Council in London, at the time the court of last resort for Canada. While Burchell argued *Imo*'s case himself before a panel of three law lords, *Mont-Blanc*'s owners wisely retained British counsel.

On March 22, 1920, the Privy Council upheld the Supreme Court of Canada's earlier decision: both vessels had equal blame for the collision.

Immediately after Judge Russell released Captain Le Médec, he returned to France via New York and returned to sea the following summer. Authorities reinstated Francis Mackey as a pilot several years later, after a change of government at the federal level. His long and hard-fought battle with the previous Conservative government was marked throughout by procrastination and the taint of guilt.

The RCN administratively discharged Acting Commander Wyatt from the navy and he moved to the United States, having been made the scapegoat for the collision and subsequent explosion.

(clockwise from left): Judge Benjamin Russell, Pilot Francis Mackey, and Evan Wyatt in 1918, after his discharge from the RCN.

Fact Sheet: Long-Time Survivors

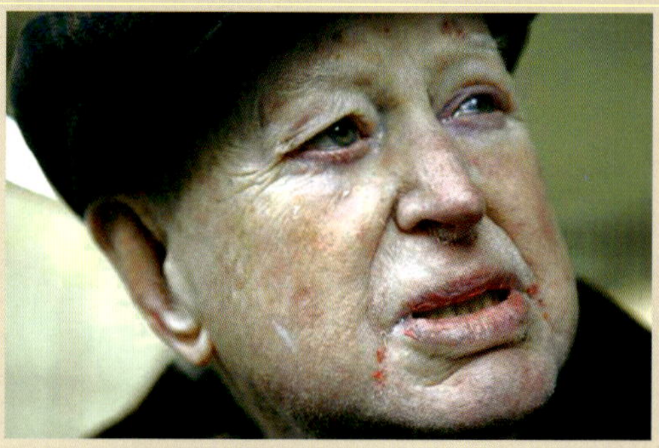

While at least 2,000 victims died at the time of the explosion and many more were to suffer premature death as a result of injuries on that horrendous day, thousands of the area's residents survived. Eventually, as the years progressed and the numbers of survivors grew fewer and fewer, there have been many claims of being the "last survivor." The poignant memories of that day by this since-departed group have helped to keep the explosion story alive for today's generation.

Although anyone who was at least 100 years old in 2017 and a resident of Halifax at the time of the explosion is technically a survivor, many of them were babes in arms without any memories of the event. Among the last survivors of the tragedy who could remember it:

Peggy Gregoire, age eight: "...when the explosion happened, we were all terrified and [the sister] brought us all out in fire drill perfect silence, nobody dared to speak a word and we came out into the school yard...middle of winter, no coats." Gregoire died in 2012 at age 103.

George Sim, six: "I was eating my breakfast when all the windows blew in. My mother was thrown in the corner with the stove on top of her and my older brother took it off of her." Sim died in 2013 at 101.

Kathleen MacDonald, six: "We lived in married quarters at...Wellington Barracks...I was blown into the bathtub and when they found me the plaster was all down over me and the soldiers dug us out, got us on transportation... My mother was three and a half days finding us." MacDonald died in 2013 at age 101.

Kathleen Davis, six: Kathleen was in her home at the corner of Jubilee Road and Walnut Street when the explosion happened. Although protected to a degree by Citadel Hill, the shock wave smashed the windows of the house, nearly killing her brother. Davis died in 2013 at 102.

Margaret Hudson, six: "All of the windows broke in the house. A soldier came and said a ship exploded...We all thought the Germans were here. They put us on a flat wagon, because there were no cars, and took us outside of the city to a farm." Hudson died in 2015 at age 103.

(images from top right) George Sim, Kathleen MacDonald, Kathleen Davis, the explosion destroyed schools, churches and other public buildings, and soldiers stand guard amid the ruins.

CHAPTER 8

THE "OTHER" HALIFAX EXPLOSION

A DANGEROUS TIME

During the Second World War Halifax once again became one of the most important Allied naval centres and convoy concentration points in the world. With the remarkable expansion of the RCN for that war, the navy had more and larger warships than in the First World War, all laden with ammunition for their weapons. These warships sailed in and out of the harbour on a virtually non-stop basis and tied up alongside the Dockyard, close to the city centre.

Convoys also formed up in the sheltered waters of Bedford Basin. They were larger, more frequent and—due to their size and cargoes of ammunition and fuel—far more dangerous than those of the First World War. The memory of the Halifax Explosion—less than three decades earlier—still loomed large in many citizens' memories.

There was a continuing fear another explosion would occur.

And it did.

But before that happened, two close calls occurred.

(right) The war according to the popular Saturday newspaper, *Star Weekly*. This colourful cover of April 3, 1943, depicts an imaginary scene of Allied warships sinking a German destroyer to protect a convoy.

(below): Spectators view the new Halifax fireboat, *Rouille*, docked at Purdy's Wharf, July 10, 1941.

TRONGATE

The SS *Trongate* makes her way up Halifax Harbour in the company off two tankers.

At 9:50 p.m. on April 9, 1942, the 6,349-tonne (7,000-ton) American ship SS *Trongate*, moored off the Halifax ferry terminal north of Georges Island, flashed a frantic signal:

"REQUIRE IMMEDIATE ASSISTANCE. FIRE BELOW DECKS."

Trongate carried 1,981 drums of highly-flammable toluene, 30 cases of filled shells, 10,474 cases of filled cartridges and 3,506 boxes of small arms ammunition. An explosion would be disastrous; the port was crammed with more than 200 ships—including packed troopships.

Initial efforts by a fireboat and tugs were ineffective and the fire spread. At 10 o'clock *Trongate* again flashed another signal:

"I HAVE TNT ABOARD."

Later signals indicated the fire was out of control and the captain intended to scuttle his ship. This was followed by a naval signal stating the minesweeper *Chedabucto* would "stand by to sink by gunfire if necessary."

Chedabucto arrived about 2:45 a.m., just as flames burst from *Trongate*'s superstructure. Sailors trained the minesweeper's searchlight on *Trongate*'s waterline, as it was crucial any shells fired hit the waterline. Any higher would not allow water to enter the hull, while lower could result in a potentially dangerous ricochet.

HMCS *Chedabucto* calmly and deliberately sank *Trongate* to prevent her cargo of ammunition from exploding on April 10, 1942.

Chedabucto's crew began to fire 4-inch practice rounds—ammunition without explosives—into *Trongate*'s hull. Despite the risk of certain death if the ship exploded, the minesweeper's courageous crew stayed at their stations, guided their vessel methodically around the burning ship and refocused the searchlight each time they stopped to fire another round.

The blazing vessel presented a spectacular scene, especially when various types of ammunition exploded and sent sparks, flames and even gold and red signal rockets arcing skywards, accompanied by the sound of incessant gunfire as small arms ammunition cooked off. Experienced sailors likened it to a night engagement at sea.

After *Chedabucto* fired about 25 rounds, the stricken *Trongate* began to settle into the water. At 3:25 a.m. she turned slightly on her side and went down in 23 metres (75 feet) of water.

Despite the extreme care *Chedabucto*'s crew took when laying their gun, one round either missed its target or went clean through the ship and ricocheted into Dartmouth, where it crashed through the roof of a business. When a woman who worked in the building came in that morning, she found the shell beside her desk as if someone had gently placed it there.

"LONG ROBBIE" TO THE RESCUE

On the evening of November 2, 1943, the 9,070-tonne (10,000-ton) American freighter SS *Volunteer* was anchored in Bedford Basin, laden with 453.5 tonnes (500 tons) of small arms ammunition, 1,632.6 tonnes (1,800 tons) of heavy howitzer shells, 2,000 barrels of highly combustible magnesium powder, a large number of depth charges, a smaller amount of dynamite and, incongruously, several large bales of tobacco.

Eighty other ships were anchored there, awaiting the departure of their convoy.

Volunteer's green wartime crew were confined onboard to protect her cargo. Bored, and with nothing better to do, a number of the ship's officers decided to play poker—and drink. The poker game progressed through the night and so did the drinking. The captain, chief engineer, chief officer and second engineer were soon intoxicated.

Dangerous cargo, raw crew, drunken officers—all the ingredients for a disaster.

It was not long in coming.

At about 5:15 the next morning, an inexperienced stoker attempted to fire up a boiler, setting the boiler room on fire. As the stoker fled to safety, the second mate, long overdue for relief by the chief mate, reported the fire to the master.

He got no reaction from him or any of the other officers, who merely continued their drunken poker game.

Confusion reigned as the fire spread and all attempts by the leaderless crew to fight it proved ineffectual.

Eventually someone succeeded in getting an SOS signal sent by wireless (initially on the wrong frequency) and signal lamp (initially in the wrong direction). After some difficulty, local naval signal stations succeeded in pinpointing *Volunteer*'s location.

They notified naval control, which dispatched a guard boat to find out what the problem was. About 10 minutes before the navy vessel arrived, *Volunteer*'s crew took to the ship's boats and headed for shore, an action reminiscent of *Mont-Blanc*'s crew a quarter of a century earlier.

Commander Owen Robertson, 36, known as "Long Robbie" because of his two-metre (six-foot, seven-inch) height, was both Commander of His Majesty's Canadian Dockyard and King's Harbour Master during the Second World War. His responsibilities included the safety of all vessels in port. He was contacted at 7:20 a.m. and rushed to his launch, waiting with six firefighters aboard. Meanwhile, the fire tug *Rouille* from the Halifax Fire Department came alongside *Volunteer* and began pumping foam into the blazing boiler room.

Robertson arrived on the scene at the same time as the National Harbours Board (NHB) fireboat *James Battle* and immediately boarded *Volunteer* to assess the situation, along with the navy's fire marshal and the NHB's fire captain. As they searched the burning ship, they soon discovered the drunken poker game, but could not get any sense out of the ship's officers.

Robertson was in a quandary; he had no authority over the master of a foreign merchant ship, but if he did not do something—and quickly—the ship and her cargo might soon be lost, or far worse.

As similarities with the Halifax Explosion crossed his mind, the sounds of bullets going off indicated the fire had reached the small arms ammunition.

He needed to act now.

Robertson arranged for the American naval liaison officer in Halifax to come aboard and formally relieve *Volunteer's* captain of his command. Then he put on an oxygen mask and an asbestos hood and set about assessing the extent of the fire.

It was worse than he expected.

Although foam had extinguished the fire in the boiler room, cargo was on fire in No. 3 Hold, threatening to explode. The most immediate danger came from eight barrels of magnesium; if they blew up, they could destroy the whole ship.

Without hesitating, Robertson entered the hold, followed by a couple of firefighters. Crawling over the top of the cargo towards the magnesium, they were engulfed by smoke from burning tobacco and cordite; small arms rounds kept popping off around them.

(left) Commander "Long Robbie" Robertson (seated, centre right) poses with American officers aboard the ice breaker USS *Burton Island* in September 1954.

(top) The fireboat *Rouille* in action. Her powerful hoses assisted in keeping the fire aboard *Trongate* under control until the ammunition-laden ship could be safely beached and scuttled.

AN EXTREME PLAN

They found eight magnesium drums, fortunately separated from each other by tobacco bales. Robertson resorted to a desperate ploy to save the ship. He directed some Dockyard welders to cut large holes in the deck above the magnesium, intending to blow the drums up one by one to vent the explosions through the holes and prevent a rupture of the bulkhead with No. 2 Hold.

While the welders worked, firefighters stacked more tobacco bales around the magnesium to protect it. They finished after an hour's heavy labour and Robertson fired into each barrel with a rifle from behind a row of bales.

It worked.

The drums went off one by one, flames roaring out through the holes in the deck above them. But two drums went off together, blowing Robertson and other firefighters about like so many rag dolls. Some were knocked out, including Robertson, while others were merely winded. One was blown right out of the hold, and later died in hospital. Those on deck quickly pulled the others from the hold and revived the unconscious ones. Although fires still burned below decks and flame and smoke billowed into the sky above the ship, the blaze was being brought under control.

The civilian crew of the fireboat *James Battle* now decided the area was too dangerous and announced they were leaving. Dishevelled, shaken, staggering, covered in black, blood trickling down his face, Robertson grabbed the rifle and yelled, "The first man who touches a line is dead!"

It worked.

By now, a Naval Boarding Party had come aboard and, just to be sure, one of its sailors was stationed on a wing of the bridge to keep an eye on things—holding the rifle.

Workmen adjust a diver's helmet before salvage begins on the cargo of a sunken ship in Halifax Harbour, July 1943.

A DANGEROUS OPTION

Robertson convened a quick council of war to consider the options: sinking *Volunteer* in situ or sinking her on the far side of Bedford Basin. Both had their disadvantages, primarily the loss of the vessel and her much-needed munitions. There was also a third option, a dangerous one that would save the ship and her cargo, but it depended on controlling the fire until the ship could reach the beaching point on McNabs Island.

It meant taking the ship through the Narrows—close to where *Mont-Blanc* exploded—passing the most heavily-populated parts of Halifax and Dartmouth. But it also meant *Volunteer* could be scuttled with her main decks above water, making her eventual salvage much easier.

The decision was made to try for Maugers Beach.

Robertson requested a harbour pilot and tugs.

When the two tugs arrived, their crews cut the anchor cable and began towing *Volunteer* with *Rouille* tied alongside, her hoses playing water into No. 3 Hold. At about 3 p.m., as the little flotilla made its way to McNabs Island, Haligonians were spared the knowledge of the drama unfolding a short distance away.

About 20 minutes later, the captain appeared on the bridge, "very, very drunk and, grabbing a megaphone, shouted at the fo'c'sle head, with nobody on it, 'Heave up the anchor!'"

Forty-five minutes later, the two tugs manoeuvred the burning vessel over a spot at Maugers Beach where she could be safely scuttled with her main deck slightly above the water. The seacocks were opened and the ship settled onto the gravel bottom, steam hissing as seawater put out the remaining fires.

The ship and most of her cargo were salvaged and, a mere three weeks later, *Volunteer* sailed for England in convoy, with a new captain and crew.

Robertson's bravery and leadership earned him the George Medal.

"...a second Halifax Explosion averted."

From the George Medal citation for Commander Owen Robertson.

Cases of salvaged goods are hoisted from a sunken freighter, July 1943.

King George's Medals

In the early days of the Second World War, existing medals did not cover the many acts of gallantry performed by civilians in Britain, particularly in relation to German air attacks. On September 24, 1940, King George VI introduced two new medals: the George Cross and George Medal. The cross was intended to be the civilian equivalent of the Victoria Cross, but awarded for acts of heroism not in the presence of the enemy, while the medal would be awarded for similar incidents, but granted more freely. While both were originally intended primarily for civilians, they could also be awarded to service personnel in cases where military medals would not normally be granted.

Only 10 Canadians have been awarded the George Cross, while 76 have received the George Medal (at right).

BEDFORD MAGAZINE

Eventually the big explosion everyone dreaded happened, but it was not during the war.

Two months after the end of the war in Europe and the disruptive V-E Day riots, a second Halifax Explosion occurred when fires and explosions rocked the Bedford Magazine.

The magazine occupied an 800-metre- (half mile-) wide piece of land along five kilometres (three miles) of the eastern shore of the basin. It consisted of a series of well-ventilated, smallish brick buildings. A berm of earth and concrete surrounded each one, designed to contain any accidental blast and force it upwards and away from its neighbours.

Masses of ammunition were stacked on the magazine's wharf from returning warships before decommissioning. The Liberal government applied political pressure to unload the ships—normally a slow process—as rapidly as possible to send their largely reservist crews home.

Many safety regulations were ignored in the name of expediency.

In particular, while the jetty should have been stacked with only one ship's ammunition at a time, often the ammunition from three ships sat there in piles up to two metres (6.6 feet) high.

The explosion that was "narrowly averted" so many times during the war was about to happen.

A convoy forms up in Bedford Basin off Africville in April 1941.

A huge mushroom cloud rises above the Bedford Magazine as stocks of ammunition stored there explode, July 18, 1945.

(opposite top): The Bedford Magazine explosion destroyed several buildings and devastated large areas of the ammunition depot.

(opposite centre): Destruction along the roadway leading to the Bedford Magazine's South Jetty.

"LONG ROBBIE" TO THE RESCUE—AGAIN

The middle week of July brought a heatwave to Halifax, leaving brush, grass and leaves highly flammable. About 6:30 p.m. on July 18, a fire broke out in a barge tied up at the magazine's South Jetty; it was widely believed to be caused by a pyrotechnic flare that leaked and then burst into flame.

One of the guards, Able Seaman Craig, spotted the fire and yelled to a mate, "I'm going down to see if I can put it out."

Craig just reached the end of the jetty when the whole structure blew up, flinging him about 180 metres (197 yards) inland.

Searchers did not find his body until three days later.

The fire quickly spread and set off a number of explosions that threatened to blow up the rest of the stored ammunition, with the potential for taking a good part of the city with it.

"Long Robbie" Robertson had just sat down to dinner with his wife in the Nova Scotian Hotel, when "there was a bang and all of the dust came out of the ventilators." He rushed to a top-floor room overlooking the harbour and saw "a mushroom cloud over the magazine!" Robertson headed for the dock, where his boat waited to take him across the harbour.

He intended to land at the South Jetty, but when he got there "the jetty had disappeared," so he landed at the North Jetty and went ashore to assess the situation.

It was not good.

About a third to a half of the older part of the dump—perhaps 160 hectares (395 acres)—was already in ruins. Robertson was put in charge of the fire-fighting efforts of all firemen, military and civilian, permanent and volunteer. Although the daytime workers had already gone home, about 200 volunteers came back.

Robertson feared the worst—a repeat of the devastating 1917 explosion. As a safety precaution, he recommended the evacuation of all Halifax residents north of Quinpool Road and those along the Bedford Highway. Thousands of residents left and several ships weighed anchor and moved out of range. Those that did not have enough time to get up steam, including vessels undergoing repairs at the shipyards, were pushed away by tugs or taken in tow by other ships.

No one wanted to chance a repetition of the 1917 explosion.

After Robertson arrived at the site, a reinforced concrete building he was standing near suddenly exploded, flinging him into a pond. With the magazine's water main destroyed in the first blast, water had to be pumped from static water tanks and a nearby stream, eventually flooding the newer magazines to prevent further explosions.

"The south end had gone. The buildings were gone. The water tower had come down with one of the first explosions."

Commander Owen Robertson, initial assessment of the Bedford Magazine explosion.

FRIENDLY FIRE

Spectators line the sidewalk outside Birks Jewellers on Barrington Street to look at glass shattered by the Bedford Magazine explosion.

As they battled the tenacious fire, exploding shells and bullets frequently drove Robertson's fire-fighting teams to the ground. Several got hit, "but all they did was make you black and blue."

The heat, heavy work and lack of water soon dehydrated Robertson and his men—plus they had no food. He got on the radio and called headquarters for food for his hungry workers. "What we would have welcomed was lettuce and ice-cream—maybe sandwiches—but good old Central Victualling Depot sent us a slab of beef and a sack of raw potatoes."

Robertson was furious.

After 24 hours without sleep he was more than a little irritable. He got on the radio again, this time on an open channel, cursed whoever was in charge of the depot and threatened to "have this guy's balls for a necktie."

Ice cream and sandwiches quickly arrived.

After two nerve-racking days of heroic efforts, Robertson again led his men to success. Damage in Halifax was largely limited to shattered windows, broken plaster, downed power lines and cracked foundations.

Miraculously, Craig was the only fatality.

Long Robbie, the man who saved Halifax from two potentially disastrous repetitions of the 1917 explosion, was simply doing his job.

Personality Profile:
"Long Robbie"

Owen Connor Struan Robertson was born in Victoria in 1907, the grandson of a famous clipper ship skipper during the golden age of sail. He was a sailor's sailor and his record of service, on both merchant vessels and warships during peace and war, stretched back to 1924. In 1932, he joined the RCN as a reservist.

After the war, Robertson commanded HMCS *Labrador*, the navy's first and only icebreaker. During her maiden voyage in 1954, *Labrador* became the first deep-draught vessel to complete the Northwest Passage and went on to circumnavigate North America.

Robertson retired from the navy in 1962 as a commodore.

Long Robbie's many achievements in the Arctic resulted in the award of the Royal Canadian Geographical Society's Massey Medal in 1961 and his appointment as an Officer of the Order of Canada—the nation's highest civilian honour—in 1970. He passed away in November 1994, at 87.

EPILOGUE

THE EXPLOSION IN POPULAR MEMORY

DEATHS IN URBAN DISASTERS

Many countries have experienced death and destruction caused by urban disasters. Most of these are due to natural causes, such as earthquakes and storms. Because such natural phenomena cover wide areas, the death toll does not necessarily reflect only urban deaths.

For example, the Great Tangshan Earthquake of 1976 recorded the greatest death toll from an earthquake in recent times. Official Chinese government statistics state 242,419 people died, but some estimates run as high as an incredible 700,000. Similarly, the Indian Ocean tsunami of 2004 did not affect only cities. It swept the shores of 14 countries and resulted in 227,898 deaths.

Deaths in urban areas caused by humans are often the result of an act of war or terrorism. The Japanese attack on Pearl Harbour in 1941 killed 2,467 people, while the 9/11 terrorist attack on New York City's Twin Towers in 2001 resulted in 2,763 deaths.

These figures pale however, in comparison to deaths from Allied bombing raids of the Second World War. Because of the destruction caused by mass bombing and the displacement of people due to the war however, exact death tolls will never be known.

Four air raids on Dresden on February 13-15, 1945, caused the highest death toll in Germany. Some 769 British and 527 American bombers dropped more than 3,500 tonnes (3,900 tons) of bombs which caused an estimated 22,700 to 25,000 deaths, although some controversial claims suggest higher.

The atomic bomb dropped on Hiroshima on August 6, 1945, probably resulted in anywhere from 50,000 to more than 100,000 dead, with 66,000 as the best estimate by Manhattan Project scientists. Although the atomic bomb dropped two days later on Nagasaki was 10 kilotons bigger (23 vs 13), it caused fewer deaths, with estimates of 35,000 to 80,000 deaths. American authorities believe it caused 39,000 fatalities.

Tens of thousands of deaths occurred later in both cities due to radiation poisoning and other injuries.

The firebombing of Tokyo on March 10, 1945, recorded the highest non-nuclear death toll in Japan, when 279 American B-29 Superfortress bombers dropped 1,510 tonnes (1,665 tons) of incendiary. According to Japanese authorities, this one raid resulted in 83,793 deaths, while post-war estimates range from 80,000 to 130,000. It was the single deadliest air raid of the war.

Despite these appalling statistics, the Halifax Explosion remains the largest single man-made, non-nuclear blast in history, but only if five criteria developed by historian Jay White are considered together: number of casualties, force of the blast, radius of devastation, quantity of explosive material and total value of property destroyed.

White has found five other explosions to rival the magnitude of the Halifax Explosion in one or more of these criteria, but none equal or exceed it in all five.

Ground Zero, Hiroshima, August 1945.

THE LONGEST-LIVED SURVIVORS?

(l-r): Frequently houses were left standing, but had one or more walls destroyed.
Hazel Forrest in 2017.

Surprisingly, no agency or organization maintains a list of the last survivors of the explosion, even for the centennial. Research has identified some of these, but it is impossible to know whether the list is complete or not, especially as some survivors moved away after the explosion.

Among those still living at the start of the explosion centennial year and who could recall events of the tragedy:

-Kaye Chapman, age five: That morning Chapman said goodbye to her four brothers and sisters as they left for school from their north end home on Clifton Street, about two kilometres (1.25 miles) from the blast site. "As young as I was, I can see everything and I can even tell you what we were dressed in. I had a little white outfit on—a tiny white dress and white stockings."

Chapman was about to play Sunday School, so picked up her Bible and hymnbook and headed outside. That decision—rather than staying in the living room—probably saved her life.

The explosion suddenly swept Chapman off her feet and she landed between the two front doors, narrowly missed by flying glass and chimney bricks. As she lay there crying, she heard her mother's screams.

Mrs. Chapman—three months pregnant—lay trapped under a buffet hutch in the kitchen. "Wherever you are, stay and don't move," her mother yelled, fearful further damage would injure the little girl. Eventually, she freed herself and crawled to her daughter.

"We just sat there and held each other for a long time."

Then, "The neighbours all come screaming out of their houses, too. We had to stand where we were because if we went outside, we would've died because everything was electrified. All you saw was people bleeding here, bleeding there or somebody holding somebody. I saw an awful lot of people holding their animals that were hurt and things like that. You know, things were that horrible. You saw that everywhere you looked, it was something bad to see."

-Hazel Forrest, six: Forrest was not at her Cork Street home that day, but staying in her aunt's apartment on Bilby Street in the north end while her father was at work. Her 36-year-old mother had died of pneumonia in June and she was recovering from a tonsillectomy, having only been released from hospital the day before.

"I was sitting by the oven door in one of these old wicker rocking chairs…and when the explosion happened the side of the house blew off…and the (exterior) steps fell down and I had to jump from the top floor down into my uncle's arms.

"We walked out Almon Street to my father's…We were only there for a little while when a Mr. Dogwell came around with a horse and a black team…He said 'Get out of the house!', everybody had to…go down the end of the street because the magazine was going to blow up…Everybody went down there and we stayed there all the rest of the day."

While her older cousin Seymour was having trouble completing his homework the night before, he exclaimed "'I wish the school would blow up'…and the next morning when he was taking his assignment to the teacher [at Bloomfield School], the [teacher's] bell…hit him in the eye...He had problems with his eye."

Forrest was also evacuated during the second Halifax Explosion of 1945. Bizarrely, she was also ill on that occasion and went to St. Margaret's Bay Road and "stayed there all night."

EXPLOSION MEMORIALS

A number of memorials in memory of the explosion are located throughout HRM.

One of the first was created by the explosion itself. The blast damaged the clock on the north face of city hall's clock tower, freezing the hands at the time of the explosion. In 1999, on the 250th anniversary of the founding of Halifax by Colonel Edward Cornwallis, the Halifax Foundation installed two replica faces on the clock. The one on the south side shows the time of day, while the one on the north face is stopped at 9:04:35—the exact moment of the explosion.

Among other early memorials were three pieces of *Mont-Blanc* mounted on pedestals, as described in the Postscript. The most prominent reminders however, are on Gottingen Street and at the top of Fort Needham Hill.

HALIFAX NORTH MEMORIAL LIBRARY

On January 14, 1954, Halifax City Council requested its Library Board prepare a report on the advisability of establishing a branch of the library in Halifax's north end. The board supported this request. Ten years later, in January 1964, the Library Board received $100,000 from the Halifax Relief Commission to support the building of the library, which would commemorate victims of the explosion. Architects Keith L. Graham & Associates were awarded the tender to design the building, which was opened in 1966 on Gottingen Street.

The previous year, the architects had commissioned a sculpture to be symbolic of the explosion and the city's rebirth after the catastrophe. The large, modernistic sculpture was made of steel, iron, bronze and wood and created by Spanish-born Quebec artist Jordi Bonet. A fragment from *Mont-Blanc* was attached to the base. The sculpture also included a bronze casting with the outline of a doll, symbolizing the hundreds of children who died. It was unveiled in 1966.

The sculpture featured an explosion of jagged metal that stood for the destruction of Halifax and vertical metal bars that represented the city's rebuilding. Those elements were among the issues that prompted the city to dismantle the work. Over the years, the sculpture had suffered damage from exposure to weather. Children loved climbing on the sculpture and a 2004 report pointed to the risk of someone slipping and being injured. The report also noted the physical decline of the sculpture and suggested reinstallation elsewhere or protected storage.

According to officials, the sculpture could not be repaired and had to be stored while its fate was decided. The sculpture was broken into pieces, which were left unmarked, and stored at various locations in the city. This decision left some in the art world shaking their heads.

When the sculpture was dismantled during library renovations, they included reconstruction of the library courtyard. The sculpture was replaced by a new work, "North is Freedom. A 2006 report by a consultant urged the city to identify the parts and bring them together. This did not happen however, and several parts disappeared, including the doll. The fragment from *Mont-Blanc* has fortunately been preserved at the Maritime Museum of the Atlantic.

In 2010, a committee of artists and citizens urged HRM to secure the surviving pieces and conduct an inventory to determine whether the sculpture could be restored and put on display in a public place. By the summer of 2011, the sculpture fragments had been brought together in a secure city storage location. But the missing centrepiece remains unlocated and is an embarrassing end to the decline of an artwork dedicated to the city's most devastating event. Jordi Bonet died in 1979 and did not live to see his work fall into decay.

The branch houses a copy of the Halifax Explosion Remembrance Book, which lists the names of the 1,951 identified victims, their ages, their local residential addresses at the time of the disaster and their subsequent places of burial. Today, Halifax North Memorial Public Library continues as a living memorial honouring the victims of the explosion.

FORT NEEDHAM HILL

Fort Needham stood on top of the highest feature in north end Halifax, a glacial drumlin similar to the hill on which the Citadel stands. Construction of the fort began in 1775, during the American Revolution, when Colonel William Spry realized the protection the hilltop could provide to the Dockyard and rearward approaches to the city.

Spry appropriated 3.65 hectares (nine acres) of James Pedley's farm and built a five-sided earthen redoubt on top of the hill, where the tennis courts are today. Later, soldiers built a blockhouse 400 metres (1,313 feet) north of the redoubt.

Soldiers manned Fort Needham during the American Revolution, the Wars with Revolutionary France, the Napoleonic Wars and the War of 1812. After the latter war, the military decommissioned the fort and left its buildings to deteriorate. By the 1880s, the army no longer needed it for the city's defence, but it still belonged to the military. British units stationed at nearby Wellington Barracks used it for training and recreation, including polo. Signs of the earthen ditch and berms were visible into the 1950s.

The Halifax Relief Commission built the current park there as a memorial to those who suffered loss in the explosion, identified by a plaque in the former rose garden. Only in 1984 was a more fitting memorial erected to commemorate the tragedy. A citizen's group raised $400,000 for the memorial tower that sits atop the hill, facing down the hillside to the exact spot where Pier 6 was located.

The tower consists of bare, narrow and angular concrete walls, punctuated by three large rectangular openings: two for bells and one for a walkway. It slopes downward from 18 metres (60 feet) at its highest point to disappear into the hill.

Taken together, these design elements suggest an image of destruction, while simultaneously evoking the energetic renewal that followed the devastation.

The bells in two of the tower's openings were originally donated to the Kaye Street United Memorial Church in 1921 in memory of the members of the Orr family who died in the explosion.

Every year on the morning of December 6, a solemn memorial service is held at the Memorial Tower. After a moment of silence, the bells ring out across the hillside and reverberate down to the water in a reverse of the blast wave that swept up the hill so many years ago.

Immediately west of the memorial, at the foot of Fort Needham Hill, the Hydrostone District stands as another visible reminder of the explosion.

Sadly, the cleared view that once existed from the memorial downhill to the location of Pier 6 has since been blocked by Irving Shipbuilding's massive fabrication shed, built to assemble the next generation of Canadian warships. The building also completely covers the location of Pier 6.

Near the northwest corner of the Hydrostone District another memorial stands in honour of the nine firemen killed responding to the *Mont-Blanc* fire. A polished black granite monument, unveiled in front of Lady Hammond Road Fire Station on the seventy-fifth anniversary of the explosion, commemorates the memory of the largest number of firefighters ever killed in Canada in a single incident.

And, as at the larger memorial atop Fort Needham Hill nearby, a ceremony is held there every December 6.

Halifax's renowned Maritime Museum of the Atlantic hosts a permanent display about the explosion, titled *"Halifax Wrecked."* It is one of the larger exhibitions in the museum and annually educates thousands of visitors from near and far about one of the world's greatest man-made disasters.

(clockwise from left): The north face of the clock on Halifax city hall is set at the exact time of the explosion.

Soldiers manning Fort Needham go about their daily tasks in this 1791 print.

"North is Freedom" replaced the explosion sculpture outside the North Branch Memorial Library.

A sculpture created to honour victims of the explosion stood outside the North Branch Memorial Library for almost 40 years before being dismantled over safety concerns.

Memorial Time Capsules

A time capsule is an historic cache of objects or information, intended to be opened at some time in the future to assist archaeologists and historians, as well as to tell the general public about life at the time the collection was deposited. Time capsules are frequently deposited during celebrations, cornerstone laying and major anniversaries.

During the memorial service in 1985, a time capsule containing a number of explosion-related artifacts was placed in an opening in the tower. The capsule is a 38-centimetre (5-inch) cube made of acid-free plastic and filled in conditions of minimum humidity. Its contents, wrapped in acid-free plastic, included both historic and modern objects.

Among the historic ones were Halifax Relief Commission forms and reports, menus from the Green Lantern Restaurant and the Halifax Hotel, names of identified dead, descriptions of unidentified dead, explosion photographs, a grocery bill and a coin.

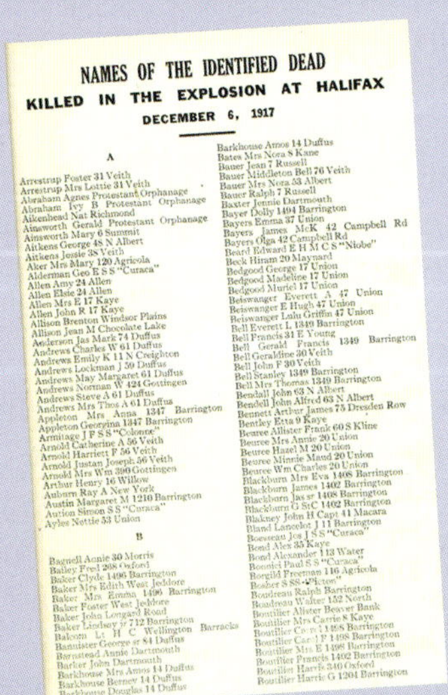
NAMES OF THE IDENTIFIED DEAD
KILLED IN THE EXPLOSION AT HALIFAX
DECEMBER 6, 1917

A

Arrestrup Foster 31 Veith
Arrestrup Mrs Lottie 31 Veith
Abraham Agnes Protestant Orphanage
Abraham Ivy B Protestant Orphanage
Aikenhead Nat Richmond
Ainsworth Gerald Protestant Orphanage
Ainsworth Mary 6 Summit
Aitkens George 48 N Albert
Aitkens Jessie 38 Veith
Aker Mrs Mary 120 Agricola
Alderman Geo E S S "Curaca"
Allen Amy 24 Allen
Allen Elsie 24 Allen
Allen Mrs E 17 Kaye
Allen John R 17 Kaye
Allison Brenton Windsor Plains
Allison Jean M Chocolate Lake
Anderson Jas Mark 74 Duffus
Andrews Charles W 61 Duffus
Andrews Emily K 11 N Creighton
Andrews Lockman J 59 Duffus
Andrews May Margaret 61 Duffus
Andrews Norman W 424 Gottingen
Andrews Steve A 61 Duffus
Andrews Mrs Thos A 61 Duffus
Appleton Mrs Anna 1347 Barrington
Appleton Georgina 1347 Barrington
Armitage J F S S "Colonne"
Arnold Catherine A 56 Veith
Arnold Harriett F 56 Veith
Arnold Justan Joseph 56 Veith
Arnold Mrs Wm 390 Gottingen
Arthur Henry 16 Willow
Auburn Ray A New York
Austin Margaret M 1210 Barrington
Aution Simon S S "Curaca"
Ayles Nettie 53 Union

B

Bagnell Annie 30 Morris
Bailey Fred 268 Oxford
Baker Clyde 1496 Barrington
Baker Mrs Edith West Jeddore
Baker Mrs Emma 1496 Barrington
Baker Foster West Jeddore
Baker John Longard Road
Baker Lindsey jr 712 Barrington
Balcom Lt H C Wellington Barracks
Bannister George sr 84 Duffus
Barnstead Annie Dartmouth
Barker John Dartmouth
Barkhouse Mrs Amos 14 Duffus
Barkhouse Berney 14 Duffus
Barkhouse Douglas 14 Duffus
Barkhouse Amos 14 Duffus
Bates Mrs Nora 8 Kane
Bauer Jean 7 Russell
Bauer Middleton Bell 76 Veith
Bauer Mrs Nora 53 Albert
Bauer Ralph 7 Russell
Baxter Jennie Dartmouth
Bayer Dolly 1494 Barrington
Bayers Emma 37 Union
Bayers James McK 42 Campbell Rd
Bayers Olga 42 Campbell Rd
Beard Edward E H M C S "Niobe"
Beck Hiram 20 Maynard
Bedgood George 17 Union
Bedgood Madeline 17 Union
Bedgood Muriel 17 Union
Beiswanger Everett A 47 Union
Beiswanger E Hugh 47 Union
Beiswanger Lulu Griffin 47 Union
Bell Everett L 1349 Barrington
Bell Francis 31 E Young
Bell Gerald Francis 1349 Barrington
Bell Geraldine 30 Veith
Bell John F 30 Veith
Bell Stanley 1349 Barrington
Bell Mrs Thomas 1349 Barrington
Bendall John 63 N Albert
Bendell John Alfred 63 N Albert
Bennett Arthur James 75 Dresden Row
Bentley Etta 9 Kaye
Beuree Allister Frank 60 S Kline
Beuree Mrs Annie 20 Union
Beuree Hazel M 20 Union
Beuree Minnie Maud 20 Union
Beuree Wm Charles 20 Union
Blackburn Mrs Eva 1408 Barrington
Blackburn James 1402 Barrington
Blackburn Jas sr 1408 Barrington
Blackburn G StC 1402 Barrington
Blakney John H Capt 41 Macara
Bland Lancelot J 11 Barrington
Boesseau Jos J S S "Curaca"
Bond Alex 35 Kaye
Bond Alexander 113 Water
Bonnici Paul S S "Curaca"
Borgild Freeman 116 Agricola
Bosher S SS "Picton"
Boudreau Ralph Barrington
Boudreau Walter 152 North
Boutilier Allister Beaver Bank
Boutilier Mrs Carrie 8 Kaye
Boutilier C[illegible] 1468 Barrington
Boutilier Carl F 1498 Barrington
Boutilier Mrs E 1498 Barrington
Boutilier Francis 1402 Barrington
Boutilier Harris 340 Oxford
Boutilier Harris G 1204 Barrington

Present-day artifacts included a video tape of a television show titled *Halifax Explosion Remembered,* a menu from Privateer's Warehouse, a grocery bill, a department store catalogue, a coin, a copy of the *Chronicle Herald* and stories of the Orr family, the bells and the memorial.

The time capsule will be removed and opened on the 100th anniversary of the explosion, at which time a new time capsule will be inserted containing contemporary items, many of them honouring the centennial of the explosion.

A CHRISTMAS TREE FOR BOSTON

The Christmas tree that Nova Scotia presents to Boston annually recognizes the assistance that city provided immediately after the explosion.

A year after the explosion, Nova Scotia donated a large Christmas tree to the city of Boston to thank the Boston Red Cross and the Massachusetts Public Safety Committee for the assistance they provided. In 1971, a second tree was sent, a tradition followed every year since.

The Lunenburg County Christmas Tree Producers Association donated the second tree, both to acknowledge the support Boston provided and promote Christmas tree exports. The Nova Scotia Government later assumed this responsibility, to continue the goodwill gesture and promote trade and tourism.

Knowing its symbolic importance to both cities, the provincial Department of Natural Resources has specific guidelines to select the tree. It must be an attractive balsam fir, white spruce or red spruce, 12 to 16 metres (40 to 50 feet) tall, healthy with good colour, of medium to heavy density, be uniform and symmetrical and easy to access. The trees usually come from open land, where they can grow tall and full, rather than from tree farms.

Before a tree is cut, each branch is individually tied to the trunk. It takes two men a day and a half to prepare the tree to be cut down. A crane holds the tree at the top while it is cut at the base by a chainsaw. The tree travels over 1,200 km (750 miles) to Boston, with a stop at the Grand Parade in Halifax for a public send-off. It then travels by truck across NovaScotia, crosses the Bay of Fundy by ferry and continues by truck to Boston.

The tree arrives in Boston under police escort. In the same way schoolchildren see the tree off in Nova Scotia, schoolchildren from Boston are on hand to welcome it to the Boston Common. Officials placed the tree at the Prudential Center from 1971 until 2002, when they moved it to the Boston Common because of a planned development.

The tree lighting usually takes place in November. Traditionally, the Nova Scotia tree is always the first tree lit on the Common. The event is broadcast live and attracts about 20,000 people.

The tree normally requires more than 3,200 man hours to decorate, as well as seven kilometres (4.5 miles) of wire and 7,000 multi-colored lights.

EXPLOSION MEMENTOES

In 2014, Halifax Regional Municipality (HRM) established an eight-person Halifax Explosion 100th Anniversary Committee to provide advice to municipal staff on the development of a civic commemorative event. As well as a major event, HRM also established a legacy capital project and a grant programme for non-profit and charitable organizations to deliver local projects in their communities.

From a number of submissions, the committee selected an emblem to symbolize the explosion's centennial. Throughout the process, committee members were careful not to characterize the emblem as a logo, due to the marketing implications associated with that word.

The Royal Canadian Mint and Canada Post also decided to commemorate the anniversary of the explosion with special issues. In the case of the mint, on February 7 it released a $100 14-karat gold coin, limited to a mintage of only 1,500. The reverse of the coin shows the stern of *Mont-Blanc* superimposed on an explosion-damaged clock face "frozen in time" at 9:04. It sells for $699.95.

As the stamp will only be issued on November 6, a month before the anniversary date, its design will not be shared publicly until then. The stamp will however, be a single self-adhesive at the permanent domestic rate, available in booklets of 10. Two million stamps will be released, in 200,000 booklets. The official first day cover will be cancelled in Halifax. It is likely that an artist's rendition of part or all of *Mont-Blanc* will appear on the stamp, along with other appropriate design elements from the explosion.

A National Historic Event

On July 4, 2016, in celebration of Canada History Week, the Minister responsible for Parks Canada announced 13 new nationally significant designations: six persons, four places and three events, all of which "helped define Canada's history." Such designations are driven by public input and are made on the recommendation of the Historic Sites and Monuments Board of Canada.

One of the three new events is the Halifax Explosion.

As noted in the federal government's press release, "The Halifax Explosion is considered by many historians to be a defining moment in Canadian history, which, for many Canadians, 'brought the war home.'"

HALIFAX
EXPLOSION
100

Santa Claus and a town crier welcome the annual Nova Scotia Christmas tree presented to Boston, November 18, 2016. It marked the first time that a tree from Cape Breton was used.

Fact Sheet: The Explosion in Fiction

The Halifax Explosion has frequently been the subject of works of popular culture—occasionally in film and on the stage—but particularly in literature. A number of adult novels have featured the explosion in their plots, sub-plots or further in the background. In chronological order:

-*A Romance of the Halifax Disaster* (1918, 1998) by Lieutenant-Colonel Frank McKelvey Bell is a melodramatic novella created by a medical officer who assisted in the rescue efforts after the catastrophic event. It follows the love affair of a young woman and an injured soldier. In addition to the story, it includes photographs of the aftermath of the disaster alongside the text.

-*Barometer Rising* (1941, 2007) was Cape Breton-born, five-time Governor-General Award-winning author Hugh MacLennan's first novel and is probably the most famous of the explosion novels. It is the story of Neil Macrae, a soldier presumed dead and accused of cowardice, who returns to Halifax to prove his innocence and reunite with his love, Penelope.

-*The Pied Piper of Dipper Creek and Other Tales* (1943) by Thomas H. Raddall contains a short story called "A Winter's Tale," which is supposedly based on the author's own experiences as a teenager during the explosion.

-*The Sixth of December* (1981) by Jim Lotz has Russian revolutionary Leon Trotsky meeting German prisoners in the Amherst prisoner of war camp. Their plotting leads to a network of enemy spies in Halifax; they cause the explosion by sabotage.

-*Burden of Desire* (1992, 2014) by journalist Robert MacNeil uses the explosion as a metaphor for the societal and cultural changes of the day and as a background to a story that is ultimately a romance. Julia Robertson, a "south-end belle" writes in her journal about her sexual fantasies. When she donates her coat to a clothing drive for those affected by the explosion, she has forgotten she hid her journal in the coat pocket. An Anglican minister finds the journal and gets his psychology professor friend to help him track down the diary's author.

-*A Wedding in December* (2005) by Anita Shreve includes a subplot about a surgeon's experiences after the explosion.

-*The Birth House* (2006), Ami MacKay's novel about midwives in early 20th century Nova Scotia, includes a section where her lead character Dora Rare travels to Halifax to offer her midwifery skills to pregnant women who go into labour after the explosion.

-*Glass Voices* (2007) by Carol Bruneau features the explosion in a story that spans decades. The story's main characters are irreversibly changed by the tragedy.

-*Black Snow: a Story of Love and Destruction* (2009) by Halifax journalist and author John Tattrie follows Tommy Joyce as he desperately searches for his wife, Evie, among the wreckage of the ruined city in the aftermath of the explosion.

-*Inherent Vice* (2009) by Thomas Pynchon includes the shadowy schooner *Golden Fang*, revealed as the re-outfitted *Preserved*, a vessel said to have survived the explosion.

-*Until I Find You* (2005) by John Irving includes a small section that refers to the explosion, although from the perspective of a modern character who visits Halifax to explore the possibility of playing a role in a film about the event.

-*Shattered* (2010) by Halifax writer Jennie Marsland is an historical romance set before the explosion and in its aftermath.

-*Dark Clouds of the Morning* (2011) by Janet C. Burrill tells the story of nurse Jennie Grayson, who leaves Halifax to look after an elderly great aunt in Truro. Her task complete, she makes plans to return on December 6, only to learn of the devastating blast.

-*Joyner's Dream* (2011, 2014) by Sylvia Tyson is the story of eight generations of a family with a knack for music and theft. It begins in England in the 1780s, continues to Halifax during the explosion and ends in present-day Toronto.

-*A Bolt from the Blue—The Halifax Explosion* (ebook 2013) by Robert James Bridge is the story of a young boy who loses all of his family in the tragedy, but despite his sad loss he goes on to become a national hero.

-*Deliverance* (ebook 2013) by Jennie Marsland is the story of Halifax-born Lieutenant Carl O'Neil, on medical leave in Canada, who vows never to return to the trenches and assumes a dead soldier's name. Out west, he meets nurse Naomi Franklin, and together they travel to Halifax before the explosion.

-*The Blue Tattoo* (2014) by Stephen Laffoley tells the story of the explosion through the lives of medical student and suffragette Elizabeth Beckett and sugar refinery worker Danny Cohen, separated by class, but pulled together by the disaster.

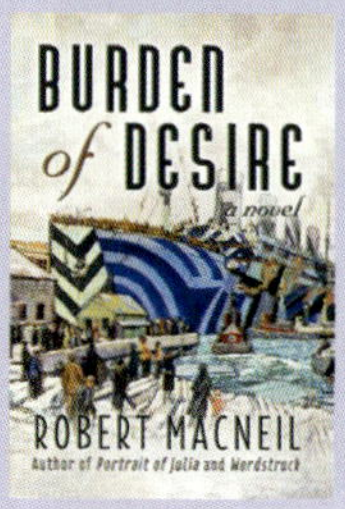

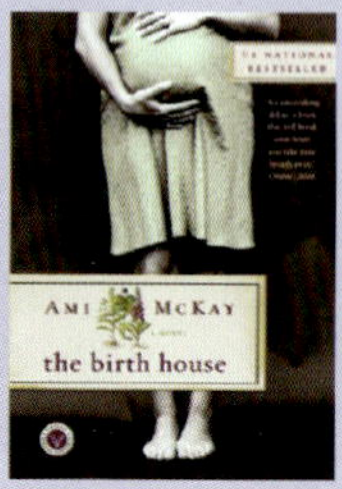

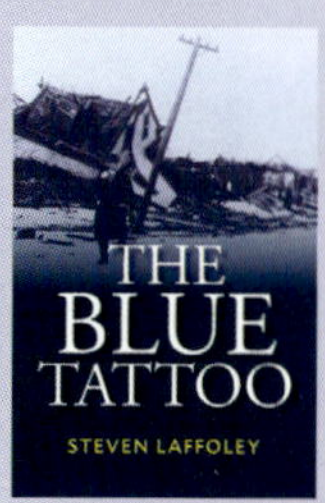

Postscript

THE BLAME GAME

A large piece of *Mont-Blanc*'s anchor shank is mounted on a pedestal at Regatta Point, not far from where it fell.

It seems in the aftermath of every human-caused disaster, someone must be blamed for it.

Who was responsible for the Halifax Explosion?

At both the macro and micro levels, two underlying issues caused the explosion: a failure of procedures and a failure of communication.

The inquiry conducted after the explosion found those in charge of *Mont-Blanc*—her captain Aimé Le Médec and her pilot, Francis Mackey and, indirectly the CXO, Acting Commander Wyatt—solely responsible for the disaster.

Yet authorities dismissed charges against all three and set them free.

A later ruling by both the Supreme Court of Canada and the Judicial Committee of the Privy Council in Britain found both vessels equally at fault.

At the macro level, the failures to follow procedures and poor communication were specifically manifested in a number of ways.

The responsible authorities did not establish effective procedures to:

- control the increase in shipping in Halifax Harbour during wartime,
- advise the CXO of dangerous cargoes aboard ships moving through or anchored anywhere in the harbour, or for him to pass this information to others who should have been advised,
- isolate ships carrying dangerous cargoes from other ships or built-up areas,
- escort ships carrying dangerous cargoes in the harbour,
- control the comings and goings of harbour pilots and for them to advise the CXO of ships' movements.

At the micro level, the same failures to follow procedures and poor communication were also manifested in a number of ways:

Rules of the Road

The "rules of the road" for ships are much the same as those for land vehicles. Generally:

- always keep to the right, or starboard, in traffic,
- signal intentions in advance, by whistles, radio, flags, loud hailers or any other means available,
- observe and respect the intentions of other vessels.

- *Mont-Blanc* proceeded up harbour on her (Dartmouth) side of the harbour at four knots, one knot under the speed limit for harbour traffic,
- *Imo* proceeded down the harbour not on her (Halifax) side of the harbour because the tramp steamer *Clara* was in her lane, at a speed some estimated at more than the seven knots, at least two knots over the maximum for harbour traffic,
- pilots aboard *Imo* and *Clara* agreed to pass starboard to starboard, when it should have been port to port,
- already out of its lane, *Imo* moved closer to the Dartmouth shore when she encountered the tug *Stella Maris* in mid-channel travelling up harbour,
- *Mont-Blanc*'s pilot, Francis Mackey, on spotting *Imo* in his channel about 1.25 kilometres (0.75 miles) away, gave a short blast on *Mont-Blanc*'s whistle to indicate he had right of way to starboard and *Imo* should move to her starboard towards the Halifax shore,
- in response, someone aboard *Imo* gave two blasts on her whistle, indicating she would not turn to starboard, but to port,

- Captain Le Médec ordered *Mont-Blanc* to stop her engines, while emitting another single whistle blast,
- in response, *Imo* once again let out two blasts,
- Le Médec then sounded two whistles and turned toward the Halifax shore,
- in a last-minute attempt to avoid a collision, *Imo* reversed engines, causing her bow to swing into *Mont-Blanc*'s side, eventually leading to the fire and explosion,
- just before the collision, *Mont-Blanc* also reversed engines,
- the crew of *Mont-Blanc* made no attempt to fight the fire—which may have been impossible in any case—but more damningly they did not try to warn any ships or other boats in the vicinity of their deadly cargo—which certainly was possible.

Curious Connection: *Imo*'s Fate

Her owners repaired *Imo* after the explosion and she returned to service. Renamed *Guvernøren* in 1920, she served as a whale oil tanker. On November 30, 1921, the captain was drunk and—with no one at the wheel—the ship crashed onto the rocks off the Falkland Islands at Cow Bay, approximately 32 kilometres (20 miles) from Port Stanley. There was no loss of life, but all salvage attempts failed and the ship was finally abandoned. Parts of her, including the anchor and pieces of anchor chain, can still be seen today. In 2005, the Falkland Islands issued a stamp with a painting of *Imo* and *Mont-Blanc* on it.

Mont-Blanc in Pieces

Several large fragments of *Mont-Blanc* survived the explosion and were found scattered throughout the area. The cannon barrel (545 kilograms; 1,200 pounds) ended up near Albro Lake in Dartmouth, a distance of 5.6 kilometers (3.5 miles) from the explosion site. Today it is located at the corner of Albro Lake Road and Pinecrest Drive, while a nearby plaque lists the names of 95 Dartmouth residents who died in the disaster.

Two large pieces of anchor shank were found. The explosion blew the bigger piece (502 kilograms; 1,140 pounds) to the far side of the Northwest Arm, 3.8 kilometres (2.35 miles) away. It sits at the corner of Spinnaker Drive and—appropriately—Anchor Drive. The smaller piece landed 3.2 kilometres (two miles) away in a marshy area near the site of present-day Calvin Presbyterian Church on Ashburn Avenue and is displayed in the church grounds. Today, these three artifacts are mounted on pedestals in memory of the disaster, not far from where they fell from the sky.

Another small and twisted metal relic of the ship—probably part of a hull plate—is cemented into a small concrete block in a park across the street from the church of St. Mother Teresa of Kolkata Parish in Halifax's north end. The church, formerly St. Stephen's, united with the former St. Joseph's Church in 2006. Next to the artifact, a granite memorial honours the seamen who sailed from Bedford Basin during both world wars, as well as to "those lives lost" when *Imo* and *Mont-Blanc* collided in the narrows "one mile east of this site." Outlines of the two ships are inscribed on the monument.

Near the water's edge at the foot of Akerley Boulevard in Dartmouth, another metal piece of *Mont-Blanc* has been used as the back of a cement garden chair. Purportedly found on the nearby grounds of the present-day Dartmouth Yacht Club, it was originally thought to be part of a propeller blade, but is now believed to be a part of her anchor, perhaps the arm (the curved, lowest part of an anchor).

Part of the upper rudder pintle (300 kilograms; 661.5 pounds) was found more than two kilometres (1.25 miles) from the explosion site. The pintle and two other large metal pieces—a portion of twisted hull plating and an identified fragment—are on display at the Maritime Museum of the Atlantic. The museum also holds several smaller pieces of *Mont-Blanc* recovered after the explosion—both metal and wood. A 13-centimetre by 14-centimetre (5.1-inch by 5.5-inch) piece of the hull is also part of the Canadian War Museum's First World War artifact collection.

Additionally, several other small pieces of *Mont-Blanc* were picked up by survivors and made their way into private homes and gardens throughout Halifax, where they remain treasured souvenirs to this day.

(top): A smaller piece of *Mont-Blanc*'s anchor shaft is mounted on a pedestal in the grounds of Calvin Presbyterian Church.

***(below)* *Imo* was salvaged and returned to service as *Guvernøren* before she was finally wrecked in 1921.**

An aerial view of Halifax and its harbour today.

Afterword

WHAT IF?

If the Halifax Explosion were to happen today and the same percentages of death, injury and destruction as the original explosion held true—based on an estimate of the 1917 population of the urban area of Halifax and Dartmouth centred on the harbour of some 70,000 civilians, soldiers and sailors, and a current population of 300,000 for the same parts of the city—it would result in approximately:

- 8,600 killed (of which 6,900 would be instant)
- 38,600 injured (of which 2,800 would be eye injuries)
- 25,700 homeless
- 81,500 with insufficient shelter.

The unprecedented recovery effort that followed the explosion formed the genesis of today's disaster relief operations.

Yet, with all our sophisticated technology, communications, transportation, rescue and recovery equipment, medical treatment and facilities, as well as emergency measures plans and exercises, could we cope with such a disaster today as well as the people of Halifax and Dartmouth did 100 years ago?

It is a sobering thought.

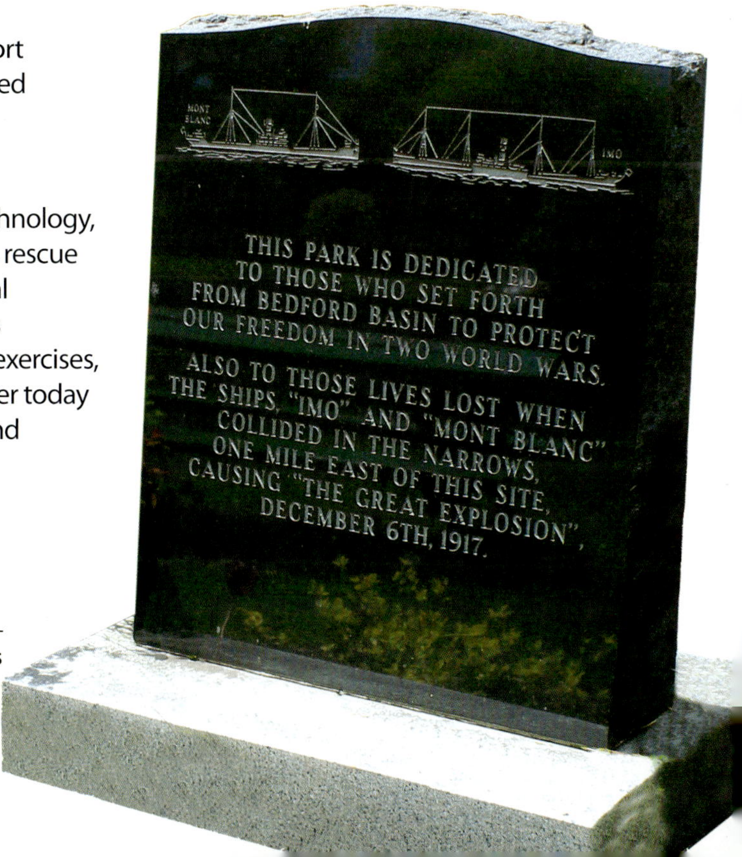

A memorial cairn in a small park across from the church of St. Mother Theresa of Kolkata Parish honours those who died in the explosion.

ACKNOWLEDGEMENTS

No work of historical non-fiction is ever written in isolation.

Any author must consult several sources—primary and secondary—to tell an effective story.

In this regard, I have been helped immensely by the many Halifax Explosion authors and researchers who have gone before me, as listed in the Bibliography. Among them, the pioneering research of Janet Kitz, the scientific and technical assessments of Allan Ruffman and his colleagues, the study of the role of the RCN by John Griffith Armstrong and the definitive account of the inquiry by my good friend Joel Zemel stand out.

I must also thank Jeff Brown, Harry Chapman, Zoltan Csepregi, Barbara DeLory, Marilyn Elliott, Lane Farguson, David Holt, Ken Hynes, Pat Jessup, Janet Maybee, Susan McClure, Vernon Oickle, Rose Poirier, Alan Ruffman, Dee Ryan-Meister. Gary Shutlak, Don Snider, Elizabeth Taylor and Craig Walkington, all of whom helped in different ways. Additionally, the expert advice and assistance that Joel Zemel provided, based on his in-depth knowledge of the explosion and the subsequent inquiry, stands head and shoulders above the rest.

The considerable talents of designer Denis Cunningham have added immeasurably to this book. Denis was enthusiastic about the project from the start; his creative handiwork is evident on every page.

A large debt of gratitude goes to my publisher, John MacIntyre, of MacIntyre & Purcell. John contacted me out of the blue and asked if I might be interested in writing a book about the explosion.

My initial response was, "What? Another explosion book?"

A few minute's conversation convinced me John had a new idea for such a book, and I was soon swept up in his enthusiasm for this project.

You are reading the result of that fortuitous phone call.

Finally—as for all my books—I must thank my wife, Miriam, who remains ever supportive of all my writing efforts.

JBB

"Lindisfarne"

Glen Margaret, Nova Scotia

June 28, 2017, 103rd anniversary of the assassination of Archduke Franz Ferdinand, which caused the First World War and led to the Halifax Explosion.

IMAGE CREDITS

Unless otherwise noted below, all images are from the author's private collection. While every effort has been made to locate image copyright owners, if any are listed incorrectly the author would be pleased to correct them in future editions.

Maps and diagrams were drawn by Denis Cunningham.

(T=top, B=bottom, L=left, C=centre, R=right).

Canadian War Museum: 12T.

City of Toronto Archives: 37, 39, 49, 52, 53T, 55T, 57BL, 62T, 63, 72L, 75, 82BC, 82B, 95L.

Halifax Chronicle Herald: 82T, 82TC, 82C.

Halifax Port Authority: 103T.

Halifax Regional Municipality: 4T, 99R.

Halifax Regional Municipality Archives: 57BR.

Hiroshima Peace Museum: 94.

Library and Archives Canada: 6, 7, 9, 12B, 13, 14 TL, 15, 16BR, 17, 34, 45, 50, 88T, 88B, 92CR, 97.

Library of Congress (Prints & Photographs Division): 31T.

Maritime Museum of the Atlantic: 27B, 41B, 44L, 44BR, 47TL.

National Portrait Gallery, London: 35C.

Naval Museum of Halifax: 54, 85B, 89B, 91T, 91C.

Private Collections: Rita Boswell: 16L;

Russell Brannon: 31B; Jeff Brown 35T;

Marilyn Elliott: 60; Janet Kitz 96BL;

Janet Maybee: 21T; Greg Murray: 29B;

Rose Poirier: 95R;

Alan Ruffman: 48B, 53B;

Dee Ryan-Meister: 14TR;

Joel Zemel: 21B, 36, 44TR, 77 C, 77B, 78C, 80, 81C, 81R, 102BR.

Public Archives of Nova Scotia: 5, 22, 25, 27T, 28T, 40, 42C, 43B, 46, 51, 57T, 58, 62B, 64, 65C, 66B, 79, 82B, 92TL.

Royal Canadian Mint: 99T.

Wikimedia Commons: 11, 32B, 35, 98R, 99B.

Yarmouth County Historical Society: 90.

BIBLIOGRAPHY

Armstrong, John Griffith. *The Halifax Explosion and the Royal Canadian Navy: Inquiry and Intrigue.*
Vancouver: UBC Press, 2002.

Beed, Blair. *1917 Halifax Explosion and American Response.*
Halifax: Nimbus, 2010.

Bird, Michael J. *The Town that Died: A Chronicle of the Halifax Explosion.*
Halifax: Nimbus, 2011.

Boileau, John. *Halifax and the Royal Canadian Navy.*
Halifax: Nimbus, 2010.

Chapman, Harry, ed. *Dartmouth's Day of Anguish.*
Dartmouth: Dartmouth Historical Association, 1992.

Erickson, Paul A. *Halifax's Other Hill: Fort Needham from Earliest Times.*
Halifax: St. Mary's University, 1984.

Fleming, David B. *Explosion in Halifax Harbour: The Illustrated Account of a Disaster that Shook the World.*
Halifax: Formac, 2004.

Glasner, Joyce. *The Halifax Explosion: Surviving the Blast that Shook a Nation.*
Canmore, AB: Altitude, 2003.

Kitz, Janet F. *Shattered City: The Halifax Explosion and the Road to Recovery.*
Halifax: Nimbus, 1989.

__________. *Survivors: Children of the Halifax Explosion. Halifax:*
Nimbus, 1992.

__________ **and Joan Payzant.**
December 1917: Re-Visiting the Halifax Explosion.
Halifax: Nimbus, 2006.

MacDonald, Laura M. *Curse of the Narrows: The Halifax Explosion 1917.*
Toronto: HarperCollins, 2005.

Mahar, James and Rowena. *Too Many to Mourn: One Family's Tragedy in the Halifax Explosion.*
Halifax: Nimbus, 1998.

Maybee, Janet. *Aftershock: The Halifax Explosion and the Persecution of Pilot Francis Mackey.*
Halifax: Nimbus, 2015.

__________.
www.pilotmackey.ca

Metson, Graham (ed.) and Archibald MacMechan. The *Halifax Explosion: December 6th 1917.*
Toronto: McGraw-Hill Ryerson, 1978.

Monnon, Mary Ann. *Miracles and Mysteries: The Halifax Explosion December 6, 1917.*
Hantsport, NS: Lancelot, 1989.

Ruffman, Alan, and Colin D. Howell.
Ground Zero: A Reassessment of the 1917 Explosion in Halifax Harbour.
Halifax: Nimbus and Gorsebrook Research Institute, 1994.

White, James F.E. *The Garrison Response to the Halifax Disaster, 6 December 1917.*
Halifax: Parks Canada, 2014 (unpublished paper).

Wright, H. Millard. *The Other Halifax Explosion: Bedford Magazine July 18-20 1945.*
Halifax: s.p., 2001.

Zemel, Joel. *Scapegoat: the extraordinary legal proceedings following the 1917 Halifax Explosion.*
Halifax: New World Publishing, 2016.